Shadow Organizations

Stefan Kühl is professor of sociology at the University of Bielefeld in Germany and works as a consultant for Metaplan, a consulting firm based in Princeton, Hamburg, Shanghai, Singapore, Versailles and Zurich. He studied sociology and history at the University of Bielefeld (Germany), Johns Hopkins University in Baltimore (USA), Université Paris-X-Nanterre (France) and the University of Oxford (UK).

Other Books by Stefan Kühl

Useful Illegality: The Benefits of Breaking the Rules in Organizations
(Organizational Dialogue Press 2022)
Organizations: A Short Introduction
(Organizational Dialogue Press 2021)
Sisyphus in Management: The Futile Search for the Optimal Organizational Structure
(Organizational Dialogue Press 2020)
The Rainmaker Effect: Contradiction of the Learning Organization
(Organizational Dialogue Press 2019)
Work: Marxist and Systems-Theoretical Approaches
(Routledge 2019)
Ordinary Organizations: Why Normal Men Carried Out the Holocaust
(Polity 2017)
When the Monkeys Run the Zoo. The Pitfalls of Flat Hierarchies
(Organizational Dialogue Press 2017)

To Contact us

Organizational Dialogue Press
Goethestraße 16
D-25451 Quickborn
Germany
Phone: +49 41 06 61 70
info@organizationaldialoguepress.com
www.organizationaldialoguepress.com

Contact the author via stefan.kuehl@uni-bielefeld.de.

Stefan Kühl

Shadow Organizations

Agile Management and Unwanted Bureaucratization

Organizational Dialogue Press
Princeton, Hamburg, Shanghai, Singapore, Versailles, Zurich

ISBN (Print) 978-1-7349619-6-6
ISBN (EPUB) 978-1-7349619-7-3

Copyright © 2023 by Stefan Kühl

Translation of Stefan Kühl's work *Schattenorganisation. Agiles Management und ungewollte Bürokratisierung* (Frankfurt, New York: Campus, 2023).

All rights reserved. No part of this publication may be reproduced or transmitted in any form or by any means, without permission in writing from the author.

Translated by: Lee Holt
Cover Design: Guido Klütsch
Typesetting: Thomas Auer
Project Management: Tabea Koepp
www.organizationaldialoguepress.com

Contents

On Supposedly New Forms of Organization,
the Crude Rehashing of What Has Already Been
Thought, and Superstitious Learning—A Foreword 7

1. On the Interest in Hyperformalized Systems— An Introduction 10

1.1 Functions of the Hyperformalization of Organizations 11
1.2 The Serendipity of a Highly Standardized Management Fashion 14
1.3 The Forms of Expectation Formation in
    Hyperformalized Organizations. 17
1.4 Two Fundamentally Different Ways
    to Design New Organizations 20
1.5 Sensitive Spots in the Treatment of Management Fashions 24

2. The Construction of Hyperformalized Organizations 28

2.1 The Thrust of Holacratic Organizations 32
2.2 The Special Form of Holacratic Formalization 38
2.3 The Peculiarities of Holacratic Formalization 41
2.4 The Bureaucratization of Post-Bureaucratic Organizations 43

3. The Renaissance of the Purposive-Rational Organizational Model 46

3.1 The Notion of Purposive-Rational Planning of the Organization 47
3.2 The Hope of Hyperformalization of the Organization 51
3.3 A More Sophisticated Variant of the Machine Model
    of the Organization 55

4.
Unintended Side Effects of the Bureaucratization of Post-Bureaucratic Organizations 57

4.1 The Pull of Formalization 58
4.2 Withdrawal Possibilities Through a Variety of Roles 61
4.3. The Reduction of Initiatives Beyond the Formal Structure 64
4.4 Attempts to Formalize Interaction 67
4.5. The Rigidity of Holacratic Organizing Principles 70

5.
Shadow Structures—Informal Correction Mechanisms in Holacratic Organizations 73

5.1 The Formation of Shadow Structures in Holacratic Organizations 74
5.2 The Thing with Transparency 79
5.3 Advantages and Disadvantages of Holacratic Shadow Structures 82
5.4 The Change Between Formality and Informality as a Competence 85

6.
On the Rise and Fall of a Management Fashion 87

6.1 On the Making of Management Fashions 89
6.2 The Outsourcing of Responsibility— on the Function of Management Fashions 99
6.3 On the Rise and Decline of a Management Fashion 104
6.4 The Alternation Between Praising the Role and Celebrating the Person 109

Methodology Epilogue 111

Bibliography 115

On Supposedly New Forms of Organization, the Crude Rehashing of What Has Already Been Thought, and Superstitious Learning—A Foreword

When we look at the discussion about "new" forms of organization, it is hard to avoid the impression that everything has been considered before. Elaborate proposals have existed for decades on how members of organizations can organize their work, how hierarchies in organizations can be abolished, and how the boundaries between departments can be dissolved. Management consultants merely sell these old, familiar ideas in new packaging and sexier language. All current management concepts, according to Drucker (2016, 19), are simply minor variations and extensions of principles for aligning organizations that have been around for over a hundred years.

Because the same ideas about self-management, the dismantling of hierarchies, and departmental permeability surface in management discourse in reliable cycles of about ten years, organizational scientists are able to determine in detail the intended and unintended effects of the concepts that are currently in vogue. Thus, thanks to research in organizational science, we know so much about the strengths and weaknesses of self-management, the advantages and disadvantages of hierarchy reduction, and the arguments for or against the formation of departments, that we can accurately assess the impact of reforms driven by management fads.[1]

For this reason, I have developed a pragmatic approach over the past decades when consultants trot out a supposedly new idea before the world of management: I take out my texts on post-bureaucratic

---

1   For reference, see my studies of post-bureaucratic organizations, through which the research literature can be accessed, in Kühl 2017; Kühl 2019a; Kühl 2020a.

organizations, some of which are decades old, replace the old terms with the new ones, and I can be sure that the analyses still apply. Often it is enough to use copy-and-paste to replace terms that now sound rather clunky, like "flexible enterprise" or "learning organization," with fresher-sounding keywords like "agile organization" or "intelligent organization." This is a very efficient way to produce a text that can easily link up with current discussions in management.

This much is certain: this crude rehashing of what has come before does not produce new knowledge. What we know about organizations is not enhanced; instead, it is merely rearranged in a new form. But as a researcher, I bear the obligation to surprise my own scholarly community with new findings, and also to perform certain hygienic functions in the practitioner discourse. When a management fad starts to overheat, there is a danger of forgetting, once again, why organizations of a certain size inevitably form hierarchies and why the differentiation of departments cannot be prevented; at such moments, organizational science's role is to remind practitioners of this knowledge.

The great danger of this approach, however, is that organizational scientists only react to management discourse. When we work with practitioners, our own willingness to learn is severely limited because every idea, every statement in management discourse, is immediately classified in terms of what came before. As a result, organizational scientists are no longer capable of perceiving new developments, because they assume that everything that is conceivable with regard to organizations has already been tried out and scientifically investigated many times. With some regularity, we observe practitioners engaging in "superstitious learning processes" that seduce us to continue thinking in the direction of a successful learning process, to refine this idea further and further, and thus to lose our openness to new things. The more often we, as organizational scientists, follow our own well-trodden paths of thought, the more convinced we are that we are on the right path.[2]

---

2 For a fundamental discussion of the process of superstitious learning and competence traps, see March and Olsen 1975; Levitt and March 1988 ; Levinthal and March 1993.

This book is the result of the painful admission of such a self-produced, superstitious learning process. The occasion for this book was the reaction to a text of mine in a major daily newspaper. I had argued that the idea propagated under the label of "agility," that trust in people—the recipe for success of "good marriages" and "good friendships"—was also suitable for the leadership of "good organizations," was naive. Instead, I pointed out that it is a central achievement of modern societies not to have to rely everywhere on trust in people. A scientist and a consultant responded to this text with the thesis that the "new self-organized forms of organization" not only rely on personal trust, but that there are "clear rules of the game" at all levels that everyone has to abide by.

My first reflex was to dismiss this as the common but meaningless "self-organized organizations need rules" formula in management discourse. But, triggered by this text, I started to take a closer look at the formalization efforts of these organizations propagated under the label of agility. And I was fascinated. In all my previous research and consulting projects on post-bureaucratic and bureaucratic organizations, I had never encountered organizations in which formal expectations had been written down in such detail. Even in state administrations, armies, and development banks, which I always considered extreme forms of formalization, I had never encountered such forms of hyper-formalization.

It therefore seemed appropriate to take a new look at organizations that I had previously filed under the label of post-bureaucracy. Whereas all the post-bureaucratic organizations I had previously examined wanted to reduce their hierarchies and dissolve their departmental silos, and engaged in a far-reaching renunciation of formalization, here I was apparently dealing with organizations that wanted to achieve hierarchy reduction and departmental dissolution through strong formalization. Could it be that a particularly bureaucratized variant of organizations was emerging under the term post-bureaucracy? If so, what makes these organizations tick, and what can we learn from them about organizations in general? This book is the answer.

1.
On the Interest in Hyperformalized Systems—An Introduction

"Your responsibility is not to support the people but to protect the process."
Brian Robertson, Holacracy (quoted from Carr 2015a)

This book is about an organizational concept that the vast majority of an organization's members have never heard of and probably never will. The concept of holacracy is touted as a solution to the crisis of hierarchy and silo formation in organizations caused by departments. Instead of occupying only one position in the organization, as is usually the case, members in holacratic organizations can take on a variety of different roles. Decision-making no longer takes place via instructions; instead, employees act independently in their roles. Instead of just being a member of a team, members can assign themselves to different circles. These circles, which operate largely autonomously, are only linked to one another via leadership and representation members, who no longer have anything to do with the classic hierarchies in organizations.

The concept of holacracy has received some attention in the discussion among consultants and managers because it promised to translate the very general notion of agility into concrete guidelines for action within organizations (an important role was played by the popularization by Laloux 2014). But even with generous estimates, one has to conclude that the concept has been introduced by a maximum of 0.0000001 percent of all organizations worldwide and abandoned by a number of these organizations after a few years. Why should we be interested in a management concept that perhaps a few hundred organizations worldwide have tried out and that quite a few have abandoned after a short time?

At first glance, holacracy is one of countless models that promise, under the label of agility, to enable organizations to respond more quickly and flexibly to constantly changing environmental conditions.³ On a superficial reading, holacracy looks like just another management fad in which consultants have stirred together almost everything that has been mentioned at one point or another in the discourse on new organizational forms. Because the ideas espoused in holacracy are, in most cases, several decades old and are rehashed in the discussions about new organizational forms that regularly resurface, it is easy to get the impression that it is just the familiar old wine in new skins.

A second glance, however, makes it clear that holacracy differs fundamentally from other management concepts traded under the term agility. While the promoters of other management systems present at best a toolbox from which organizations can select the tools that are right for them, holacracy is propagated as a closed organizational concept in which the individual elements are precisely coordinated. The elements interlock so precisely, at least according to the concept's promise, that a new type of organization can be created without silo formation and without hierarchy.

1.1 Functions of the Hyperformalization of Organizations

Holacratic organizations use a clever trick to achieve the dissolution of departmental boundaries and the softening of hierarchies: A detailed formal fixation of all conceivable expectations of organizational members. Every assumption of a task, every assignment to a circle, every shift of responsibilities, no matter how small, is fixed in the organization's control software for all to see. This creates a multitude of detailed role descriptions for all organization members, which can be combined into comprehensive individualized job descriptions. Even in holacratic

---

3   See, as just one example of the myriad proposals for supposedly new forms of organization, Wolfe 2011; Torbert 2004; Taylor and LaBarre 2006; Sisodia, Wolfe, and Sheth 2010; Kofman 2006; Mackey 2013; Hock 2005; Hamel 2007; Hamel and Zanini 2020; Collins 2001; Block 2013; Benefiel 2005; Barrett 2013.

micro-organizations with barely a dozen employees, job descriptions of thirty or forty tightly described pages can quickly emerge for each individual organizational member. Given this explosion of formal rules, holacratic organizations resemble their frequently criticized large-scale bureaucratic counterparts (see as a sampling of such criticism Urwick 1943; Crozier 1963; Graeber 2015).

But at one point there is a fundamental difference. While in classic bureaucratic organizations the change of formal structures through the reorganization of departments or the redefinition of processes is often a lengthy process, the formal structures of holacratic organizations are in a constant process of change. Each individual member of the organization can adapt his or her own role descriptions to current requirements at any time, even without consulting other members. In each steering meeting of a circle, new circles can be formed, new roles defined, or new responsibilities and rights determined. This creates a formal order that, unlike in classic bureaucratic organizations, is in a permanent state of flux.

The formal order of holacratic organizations is protected by the fact that organizations commit to holacratic principles by signing a nearly fifty-page "constitution" that lays out all the details of how an organization is governed (see Robertson 2015b, 23).[4] This interlocking of the elements specified in the constitution is done by holacratic governance software, which maps all of an organization's formal communication and decision-making processes. Although organizations can forego the use of these software packages, from a size of at least twenty or thirty employees the complexity becomes so great that holacratic organizations can hardly be controlled without this technical support.[5]

This fixing of expectations for organizational members down to the smallest detail can be called *hyperformalization*.[6] Formalization in

---

[4] The exact number of pages depends on the version and the font. The German variant of version 5.0 comprises just under 40 pages (Xpreneurs 2021), the English variant of this version with very small typesetting a little over 20 pages (HolacracyOne 2020)

[5] The emergence and role of holacratic software packages such as glassfrog or holaspirit has not yet been studied in detail.

[6] The term hyperformalization has been used primarily to refer to processes of personnel selection. See Noon et al. 2013.

organizational science refers to the attempt to set expectations that members of an organization must meet if they are to remain members of an organization (Luhmann 1964, 38). Building on this, hyperformalization can be defined as the effort to formally set every expectation in an organization, no matter how small (see also Sua-Ngam-Iam and Kühl 2021, 55f.).

Every organization—and this idea from organization science is central—depends on a certain degree of formalization. Even in associations, citizens' initiatives or political parties, in which most members not only work without pay but often even pay for their membership, there is a minimum of formal expectations that one has to meet in order to remain a member of the organization. Companies, administrations, or hospitals, which usually pay their organizational members, are only able to act at all because they can expect their staff to comply with formal rules, with the support of implicit or explicit references to the possibility of termination. Holacratic organizations take this concept of formalization, which governs all organizations, to an extreme.

It is precisely this form of hyperformalization that is interesting for organizational scholars, because it allows us to observe not only the functions but also the consequences of formalization, as if under a magnifying glass. Admittedly, there have always been such attempts at hyperformalization in organizations. Just think of the management concept of Taylorism, in which the aim was to establish a perfect formal structure (see Taylor 1967; for criticism e.g. Wood and Kelly 1982), or the Harzburg model, now largely forgotten, in which an attempt was made to decentralize responsibilities by means of an extensive constitution and detailed job descriptions (as a starting point, see Höhn 1966; for criticism, e.g. Guserl 1973; Grunwald and Bernthal 1983), or Business Process Reengineering, which also disappeared into oblivion, in which processes were formalized in detail with the support of control software (as a starting point, see Hammer and Champy 1993; for criticism, Knights and Willmott 2000). Despite all similarities, however, no organizational model has taken formalization to such an extreme as holacracy.

I want to focus here on the construction and effects of holacratic organizations. The holacratic model illustrates basic things about organizations that struggle with the unintended side effects of forming hierarchies and differentiating departments. Management models that take individual organizational principles to the extreme are helpful as illustrative subjects for understanding the functions and consequences of basic organizational ideas.

1.2 The Serendipity of a Highly Standardized Management Fashion

There is broad interest in organizational concepts because they successfully establish themselves as management fashions, which are widely shared ideas about how companies, administrations, hospitals, universities, schools, armies, police forces, or associations can be better organized. They address the widespread need in organizations to remedy perceived deficits and to tap previously unused opportunities for improvement. In this context, management fashions suggest that the introduction of new design principles can increase adaptability, performance and innovation (see Carson et al. 2000, 1143f.).

The term "fashion" implies that organizations are "infected" by the concept currently in vogue. Similar to clothing fashions, there are also pioneers in organizational fashions, which are then followed by many others (see Aspers 2005). It is impossible to know who the pioneering fashionista is, but as soon as one emerges, more and more people follow his or her lead. A process of "social contagion" takes place from which it is increasingly difficult to escape. At some point, the social pressure is so strong that you have to justify why you are not (depending on the current fad) lean, digital or agile.

When a new management fashion surges up in the business press, management journals, and executive conferences, many organizations often have no choice but to adapt to these management fads in some way (on so-called "isomorphism," see DiMaggio and Powell 1983). We know from organizational research that the survival of many organizations is not solely influenced by their capabilities in producing products, delivering services, or teaching pupils or students, but depends significantly on their legitimacy in their relevant environment (see the classic Meyer and Rowan 1977). In this respect, it makes sense for organizations not only to commit to generally accepted values such as environmental protection, human rights, diversity, or gender equality, but also to position themselves as innovative and flexible organizations (see in detail Meyer 1992). Adaptation to current management fashions, even if merely verbal in nature, plays an important role here.

In many cases, symbolic measures on the display side of organizations can satisfy environmental requirements. The communications department sets up a new mission statement process, the human resources development department purchases new training, and the quality assurance department adjusts its observation grids. Certainly, such measures do not pass the organization by without leaving a trace, but in the rarest of cases there are immediate effects in the form of fundamentally changed formal expectations. The display side of the organization, which serves to produce legitimacy, and the formal side remain largely decoupled (on this concept, see Kühl 2013, 132).

This form of decoupling of the display and formal sides, which is common for management fashions, does not actually take place in holacratic organizations. The attempt to patent the concept of holacracy aims not only to monetize the concept comprehensively, but also to fix the formal framework for the applying organizations.[7] The principles set by a holacratic constitution are so strongly fixed that any change is immediately codified as a formal expectation. This process is intensified by the fact that the holacratic governance software leaves little room for deviation in the formal structure. Holacratic organizations—unlike many other organizations that adapt to management fashions—do not

---

7   See the patent application United States Patent Application Publication US 2009/0006113 A1; the web address can be found in the bibliography in Robertson, Moquin, and Powell 2009. The aim of the patent application seems to have been to control the development of holacracy and furthermore to be able to charge fees for the use of the holacratic organizational concept. However, holacracy was then stopped by the U.S. Patent Office with the indication that organizational concepts cannot be patented in principle (on the difficulties with the patenting of the concept, see Groth 2018b, 113). After the failure of the patent application, it was only possible to protect holacracy under trademark law.

primarily change their external appearance, but they do change their formal structure in particular.

The introduction of holacratic structures is intended, at least, to lead all employees to speak the "same language." Going further, the vision anticipates that by adopting holacracy, large corporations, innovative startups, and small businesses would have a common ground of understanding through which they could share ideas, exchange talent, and innovate (at least, that is the vision for a network of companies in Las Vegas where holacracy has been introduced; see Groth 2018b, 69). It takes a certain tolerance for frustration to understand the complex principles of holacracy. Once you understand them, however, you can easily move from one holacratic organization to the next.

For organizational researchers, the high degree of formal standardization of holacratic organizations is a stroke of luck. Studies of new organizational forms suffer from the fact that hardly any organization is like another. Sometimes the implementation of supposedly revolutionary management principles are merely minor efforts in a few departments, largely isolated from the rest of the organization. Occasionally, organizations see themselves as agile pioneers simply by eliminating one or two levels of hierarchy and setting up a few cross-departmental project teams without changing anything in the basic principles of their own organization. Identifying the common characteristics of organizations that advertise themselves as pioneers is often like trying to nail a pudding to the wall.[8]

This problem does not come up in holacratic organizations. Holacratic organizations all function according to a precisely defined blueprint, which makes structural effects in various holacratic organizations very similar. Within the holacratic principles, organizations can permanently change the configuration of roles or circles; but deviations from individual holacratic principles require changing the constitution—then valid for all holacratic organizations—and subsequent adaptation

---

8   Researchers, evading this complexity, often focus only on a post-bureaucratic ideal type (see, for examples only, Heckscher 1994, 15ff.; Grey 2013, 81).

of the control software. To exaggerate: If you know one holacratic organization, you know them all.

From an organizational science perspective, holacracy can be understood as a grand "experiment" in which generalizing statements become possible through the introduction of a highly standardized management concept in various organizations (such as Hodge 2015; Groth 2018b, 68f.). Given the high degree of standardization, the setting resembles classic social psychological experiments such as the Milgram experiment, which tested organizational members' willingness to follow instructions (Milgram 1974); the Stanford Prison Experiment, which demonstrated the effect of role assignment on violent behavior (Zimbardo 2007); or the Robber Cave Experiment, which demonstrated how easily conflict can arise between groups (Sherif et al. 1988). While members of holacratic organizations can only choose to participate in the experiment to a limited extent, it is a unique opportunity for organizational scholars because the effects of hyperformalization can be observed very closely in these highly similar organizations.

What organizational science tools are available to understand this experiment in hyperformalization of organizations?

1.3 The Forms of Expectation Formation in Hyperformalized Organizations

Every analysis of an organization—and, indeed, every analysis of groups of friends, small families or protest movements—starts with an examination of the way in which *expectations* are formed. This focus on the formation of expectations may be surprising, but this is the only way to understand how social structures stabilize in the first place. Only through expectations do we know what behavior a counterpart is likely to display and what behavior, on the other hand, the counterpart expects from oneself.

The emergence of expectations in relations can proceed largely without presuppositions. It is "a primitive technique pure and simple" (according to Luhmann 1995, 323). One can test whether or not the need for a good conversation, for a close friendship, or for a sexual relationship is shared. Through the fulfillment or disappointment of initially spontaneously formed expectations, one then gradually develops certainty of expectation. At some point, one knows that one cannot expect good conversation when a colleague is stressed, that one should not articulate the demand for a close friendship to complete strangers, and that the initiation of sexual relations is based on the correct interpretation of the other person's signals.

Of course, one can always try to figure out for oneself which spontaneously formed expectations will stand the test of time and which will be disappointed. But at some point in childhood, we discover that there are expectations in society that we can assume are more socially supported than others (see Luhmann 1995, 324). You learn that biking naked around town is not tolerated, but that nudity in your own home is normally accepted.[9] These expectations become more and more refined until we understand that the right to nudity in one's own four walls is restricted when visitors are present, or that with nudist beaches there are public places where nudity is not only accepted but even expected, even though strict norms still apply as to where one is allowed to look.[10]

When we examine organizations, different forms of expectation formation come to mind (see Luhmann 1985, 64; Luhmann 1995, 368). In an organization, expectation formation takes place through values and programs as well as through roles and people, and we have to describe the interplay of these forms of expectation in order to understand an organization in detail. If we were to view organizations only as a value-based entity, only as a collection of super-personal programs, only as a set of role-bearers, or only as an accumulation of staff or people, we would merely get a highly distorted picture.

---

9 Students at Bielefeld University were able to observe this for a long time in a real-life experiment by Ernst Wilhelm Wittig—known as Ernie—who regularly biked naked through Bielefeld, showed up to seminar events undressed, and went to the soccer stadium only wearing a cap.

10 On the formation of expectations on beaches, see Kaufmann 1996.

Values represent the most abstract form of expectation formation in organizations. They are ideas of what is desired that are reflected in the choice between alternatives for action but do not provide clear criteria for right and wrong behavior (Friedrichs 1968, 113). Popular values in organizations are sustainability, diversity, innovativeness, efficiency, appreciation or transparency. They are so abstract that they are well suited for the front page and can easily be written into the mission statement of almost any organization, but they do not specify what concretely follows from them.

In contrast to values, *programs* in organizations form clear criteria for right or wrong decisions (see Luhmann 2018, 210ff.). The sales goals in a company, the procedure for issuing a passport by an administration, or the application for travel reimbursement in universities are specified so precisely that a distinction can be made between correct and incorrect behavior. Working from programs, an organizational member can very accurately guess whether a law is being broken, a formal rule of the organization is being violated, or an informal norm is being violated, even when taking into account all the available room for interpretation.

While programs function independently of people, *roles* in organizations can only be exercised by specific people. A role is understood as a bundle of expectations that are attached to the behavior of the bearers of positions. Thus, it is a matter of expectations that "a person can perform," "yet that are not fixed to specific people," but are rather "exercised by different, possibly changing role bearers" (Luhmann 1985, 67f.). We expect a policeman—at least in a democracy—to rush to our support when we are threatened by a criminal. Which exact policeman does not matter for the formation of expectations. In the case of roles, the expectation is not linked to a specific person, but rather to a bundle of expectations summarized in a role.

The formation of expectations about people can be distinguished from the stabilization of behavioral expectations about roles. We know intuitively that what we have experienced with one person cannot easily be transferred to experiences with another individual. In order to develop expectation stability about people, we need to have experienced them in a series of situations in which they could present themselves with all of their particularities. Naturally, expectation stabilization via knowledge of persons plays an important role, especially in romantic couples, small families, and friendship groups. But it also works in organizations. One quickly recognizes that people in the same position behave quite differently, and the assessment of different job holders' personalities enables us to know more precisely what to expect.

Different forms of expectation formation are also found in holacratic organizations. No holacratic organization does away with the usual commitments to values such as participation, sustainability, and mindfulness (see Robertson 2015a, 31ff.). The constitution, which must be signed by all holacratic organizations, is a collection of programs used to determine right and wrong actions within holacracy. Roles are identified in this constitution as a central element of holacratic organizations and play an important role in the form of comprehensive job descriptions for each individual member of the organization. But with all the focus on roles, it is of course impossible to prevent the formation of expectations about people, even in holacratic organizations.

But in holacracy, there is a clear focus on expectation formation. If we were to describe the holacratic concept in the most succinct form imaginable, it is this: the dream that programs cast in a rigid constitution will make it possible to achieve behavioral expectations in organizations, to the greatest extent possible, through precisely defined role expectations. This aspiration has been dreamed again and again in organizations for over a hundred years, but holacracy pursues it in an almost purely idealized form.

What makes holacratic organizations so interesting to researchers studying new forms of organization?

1.4 Two Fundamentally Different Ways to Design New Organizations

If you look at the discussion about new forms of organization, you first have to wade through semantic garbage, both as a researcher and as a practitioner. Attempts to define post-bureaucratic organizations via the fashionable word of agility are often nothing more than a collection of decent-sounding lists of values. For a company, agility, according to just one swaggering example, means the ability to operate profitably in a competitive environment characterized by constant as well as unpredictable, changing customer demands (Bottani 2010). The idea of agile management describes—in another case study of how to string together meaningless words—a flexible and lean, innovative as well as customer-oriented, employee-competence-based organization relying on new technologies, which recognizes market developments at an early stage and adapts quickly in terms of structures and processes as well as people and culture (Gunasekaran 1998).

As with all lists of values, an accumulation of sonorous vocabulary creates an effect of high-consensus certainty (Luhmann 2018, 196). Who does not want their company to have the ability to operate profitably in a competitive environment? Who doesn't want to have an organization that is flexible and lean, innovative and customer-focused, employee-competence-oriented and based on new technologies, that recognizes market developments early on and adapts quickly in terms of structures and processes as well as people and culture? This string of discursive ringtones is therefore suitable for the approval-seeking Sunday speeches of a CEO or managing director, but they don't really offer any clues about what exactly is taking place in organizations.

In the process, the semantic flotsam and jetsam in management discourse produces a devastating effect. The celebration of euphonious catalogs of values overlooks the fact that—and this idea is essential—two fundamentally different conceptions of organizations have developed in the shadows with abstract terms such as agility and flexibility. One notion seeks to achieve efficiency, effectiveness, and innovation through maximum formality, while the other relies on maximum informality to achieve these goals.[11] If we adopt the preference in management literature for single-letter model names—"Model X,"

---

11 See also the evaluation of the case studies of Zappos and Valve by Lee and Edmondson 2017, 54.

"Model Y," or "Model J"—we can take a look at a "Model F" and a "Model I."

In *"Model F"*—the Formality Model—the goal is to formally fix the highest possible number of behavioral expectations for organizational members via precise role definitions. The formula for success entails an ever further detailing and perfecting of formal role expectations. The existence of informal expectations in organizations tied to people is noted, but efforts are made to translate as many of these as possible into formal role expectations. People, to borrow from a traditional metaphor, are expected to function like cogs in the organization's machinery. The metaphors used for this organizational model are then also mechanistic in character: machine, mechanism, apparatus, or operating system (see Morgan 1986, 19ff.).

In contrast, *"Model I"*—the Informality Model—relies on the fact that as many expectations as possible are formed informally in organizations on the basis of trust in persons (see for example Toffler 1971; Mintzberg and McHugh 1985; Peters 1993; Ciborra 1996). The formula for success consists in resisting the urge to formalize behavioral expectations ever further in ever more detailed role descriptions. The necessity of formal role expectations is not negated, but these should only provide a framework for informal expectations based on personal trust. People are supposed to be at the center of the organization. The metaphors used for this organizational model are organism, community, lifeworld, or culture (see Morgan 1986, 39ff.).

Ever since scholars have examined organizations, the emphasis has been on either the potentials of formality or the potentials of informality (see Krell 1991, 149 and much later Adler 2003, 353ff.). Although it may be an exaggeration to say so, the history of management concepts can be described as a back-and-forth shift not only between the dismantling and reduction of hierarchies or between the differentiation or dissolution of departmental boundaries, but also between formality and informality.

In this context, Taylorism at the beginning of the twentieth century was certainly the first prominent attempt to achieve efficiency advantages by extensively formalizing organizational roles with if-then rules, which are also called conditional programs.[12] The post-World War II models of leadership in the employee relationship, or leadership via goal agreements, then broke away from the idea that organizational members should be led by conditional programs that were as precise as possible. However, these systems continued to rely on the possibilities of formalization, in this case by defining precise goal programs for all roles in the organization.

Organizational concepts based on the formation of informal expectations have repeatedly emerged as a reaction to attempts at far-reaching formalization (on community concepts, see Adler and Heckscher 2006). At the beginning of the twentieth century, the idea of a factory community emerged, in which the emphasis was placed on the formation of collegial expectations tied to specific people in the completion of tasks (on radicalization in the form of National Socialist factory communities, see also Eden and Möbius 2020). Then, in the second half of the twentieth century, models of "communalizing personnel policy" emerged, in which the importance of the person was placed at the center of the formation of expectations (Krell 1994, 12ff.). These received considerable attention first in Japan, then in the USA, and finally in Europe under the concept of organizational culture.

Although many initially suppose that post-bureaucratic organizations have a low degree of bureaucratization, any discussion of new organizational forms seems to include concepts that focus either more on formality or more on informality. On the one hand, there are models that seek to reduce hierarchies and soften departmental boundaries by emphasizing informal expectation formation tied to people. The agile manifesto summarizes these ideas succinctly as "individuals and interactions are more important than processes and tools" (Beck et al. 2001). Such an approach focuses on human resources, in the hope that personnel can cooperate with each other, unencumbered by formal rules (for radical models, see Hastings and Meyer 2020 or Hamel and

---

12 One could, of course, also think of other variants of organizations strongly oriented towards formality. See for example the considerations of Harrington Emerson (1924), who in his "Twelve Principles of Efficiency" took the overall goal of the organization as a starting point more strongly than Taylor.

Zanini 2020). On the other hand, however—contrary to what the term post-bureaucratic organizations might suggest—there are also approaches here that aim to reduce hierarchies and soften departmental boundaries by formalizing role expectations to a greater extent. Holacratic organizations are only the most radical variant, in which a kind of "agilization" is sought through a detailed definition of formal roles (for other models, see for example Lee and Edmondson 2017; Kates et al. 2021).

Both in research and in practice, we know a great deal about organizations that attempt to reduce their hierarchies, soften their departmental boundaries and downgrade their formal requirements under the label of post-bureaucracy.[13] However, findings remain slim in both research and practice regarding organizations that attempt to flatten hierarchies and loosen up departmental boundaries while at the same time hyperformalizing the organization. Understanding the process of hyperformalization more precisely is the central concern of this book.

1.5 Sensitive Spots in the Treatment of Management Fashions

When dealing with a management fashion, we are inevitably venturing into dangerous territory. Especially at the beginning, we find euphoric representatives who see the philosopher's stone in the management fashion they are promoting. Not only the inventors of a management fashion play a role in this, but also consultants who earn their money with the introduction of these organizational concepts, as well as managers who tie their careers to the integration of a management fad in their organization. However, at the latest, when the first practical experiences with an organizational concept are available, the first critics

---

13 As a "classic" on post-bureaucratic organizations, I would refer to Heydebrand 1989, Manz and Sims 1980, Cafferata 1982, Heckscher 1994, Grey and Garsten 2001. See for my own work Kühl 2017; Kühl 2019a; Kühl 2020a. An overview can be found at Alvesson and Thompson 2005.

also chime in and point out the blind spots. Then these concepts are gradually replaced by new management fashions.

Thus, it is not surprising that holacracy also has both staunch advocates and sharp critics (see Rąb-Kettler 2018, 171f.; Ravarini and Martinez 2019, 63ff.). For supporters of the concept, holacracy is nothing less than the *"revolutionary management system that abolishes hierarchy"* (Robertson 2015b, 3). "The vibrant city of Holacra City" would, according to the flowery imagery of dyed-in-the-wool holacrats, finally fill the gap that has arisen between the "companies that have settled on the level of self-organization" "along the Purpose River" as well as the "software companies from the Highlands of Agility" (Bernardis et al. 2017, 10).

Critics, on the other hand, point out that holacracy is too bureaucratic, too process-oriented, too rule-heavy (Denning 2014; Veuve 2017). In holacracy, processes are placed above people and thus ultimately organized without regard to people's interests (Appelo 2016). The complicated set of rules is criticized, which is not intuitively comprehensible, but must first be painstakingly learned by employees (Caddell 2016; Bernstein et al. 2016; Zeuch 2016b). Especially when it is necessary to communicate quickly between different functions in an organization, the highly regulated system bumps up against its limits (Oane 2016; Doyle 2016).

For organization scholars, these controversies between euphoric proponents and strident critics are interesting as empirical material. However, there is little reason to take one side or the other. Any measure to design communication channels, define programs, or select personnel is introduced with the hope that it will perform important functions for the organization. At the same time, however, we also know that these measures cannot avoid unintended side effects (for more on this, see Merton 1936, 894). Every "solution for a problem" inevitably has "problems with the solution" (Luhmann 1964, 382). The optimal organizational structure may shape the dreams of some practitioners; in reality these structures do not exist.

But despite all the distancing, as a scholar one cannot avoid being drawn into the controversies. Even the use of the subjunctive triggers irritation among particularly diehard advocates of management concepts. At the latest, the analysis of a management concept as a management fad frequently elicits audible gasps. As soon as a researcher deconstructs the implicit organizational understanding of a management concept, points out unintended side-effects or unintended structural effects, or describes informal evasive movements, he or she inevitably draws strong reactions from a concept's supporters.

The reactions of a management concept's advocates are always the same. Their descriptions purport to be based on original ideas, while they do not pay sufficient consideration to the fundamental further developments of the concept. They would lodge the accusation that you haven't fully grasped the concept because you haven't yet personally experienced it in its full application. Their criticism would be based on analyses of organizations that have not yet reached the necessary level of maturity in introducing the management concept. Observations in individual organizations would be overly generalized and divergent experiences of other organizations—especially one's own—would not be sufficiently taken into account.

As an organization scientist, one could avoid these disputes with practitioners by writing only for the echo chamber of sympathetic scientific colleagues. Publication in a scientific journal guarantees that hardly any practitioner will take note of these reflections. After all, one would have to scan the relevant scientific journals, obtain the article from a university library and then delve into a theoretically dense text. If researchers write primarily for other researchers, they can rest assured that no practitioner will be upset about their academic thoughts; but then they also have to live with the fact that their writings will find no relevance outside of academia.

This book may be unusual in that it deliberately attempts to bridge the gap between organizational science and organizational practice without attempting to resolve the fundamental tension between these two fields. As a result, both organization scholars and organization practitioners are in for a treat: organization scholars are confronted with a rather unusual form of presentation. This book is based on empirical research that is presented in detail elsewhere in journals and edited volumes (see, for example. Sua-Ngam-Iam and Kühl 2021; Kühl and Sua-Ngam-Iam 2023), whereas detailed theory discussions, methodological expositions, and case presentations are largely omitted here. But I can guarantee that organizational scholars will find one or two interesting things to think about. Organizational practitioners, on the other hand, will be required to confront a rather unfamiliar picture of organizations. The emphasis on unfamiliar side-effects and unintended structural effects does not fit the picture that practitioners normally have of organizations. My hope, however, is that the descriptions presented here will ultimately be closer to practitioners' perceptions of reality than the usual management books that are trimmed down to make for a compelling read. If, at the end of reading this book, you gain an even more accurate sense of how organizations function as a whole, beyond the effects of hyperformalized organizations—then all the better.

2.
The Construction of Hyperformalized Organizations

> "When you're all tied up,
> that's when you can actually free your mind."
> Aimee Groth, comparing the effect of holacracy with
> the principles of Shibari, a Japanese bondage art (Groth 2018b, 159f.)

The interesting thing about the real-world experiment in holacracy is that, contrary to the general trend toward increasing an organization's human qualities, it relies on the formation of expectations via roles. Roles, as holacrats understand it, are "*the* fundamental building blocks" in the structure of an organization. Rights, according to this conception, are distributed "not to individual people" but to "roles." These roles would merely be "energized" by employees (Robertson 2015b, 38, italics in original). In this context, roles are understood in the language as an "organizational construct" that is "exercised" by a person in the "sense of the organization" and is "energized" by them (HolacracyOne 2020, 1.1).

Roles are therefore the primary starting point for holacrats to shape organizations (Laloux 2014, 118).[14] Organizations, according to holacrats, are "not about people." There is no attempt "to make people better or to make them more compassionate or aware." Nor is there a "demand that a particular culture be created" or that "people come into a particular relationship with each other." Rather, holacrats believe that the "conditions are created in which personal or cultural development can unfold naturally—or not, if it is not to be" (Robertson 2015a, 165).

---

14 Frederic Laloux notes: "One of the core elements of holacracy, which can be found in all Teal Organizations in this research, is to separate role from soul, to break the fusion of identity between people and their job titles. In holacratic language, people don't have a job, but fill a number of granular roles." (Laloux 2014, 119).

Now, taking on a role in an organization is nothing special to begin with. When a new member joins an organization, he or she is assigned a specific role, whether it be manufacturing tooling parts, leading an assembly team, or responding to incoming inquiries. In the process, these assigned roles can change through task modifications, transfers to a new team, or by moving up the hierarchy. What is unique about holacracy is that employees can take on a whole range of different roles anchored in different parts of the organization. Each member of the organization—holacracy terminology describes members as partners—assembles their own role potpourri.

Each individual role of this potpourri is defined in detail via objectives, areas of responsibility, and tasks. Objectives loaded with meaning—also called "purposes"—describe why the role exists and what it aims to achieve. An area of responsibility—a "domain"—defines the role's area of sole authority. The tasks of the role—the "accountabilities"—define the goals to be achieved with this role (see HolacracyOne 2020, 1.1; see also Robertson 2015b, 42f.). The role task is thereby declared a "sacred task" for each role owner. Like mothers or fathers charged with the education of their children, role carriers have to take care of a task in the holacracy. A role bearer's fulfillment of tasks therefore have to follow "an act of love and service" not for the own well-being, but for the well-being of the organization and from the "free will" of the role bearers (Robertson 2015a, 75).

When an organizational member fills a role, that member is given "the authority to take any action" that he or she deems useful as a role bearer to "express the role's purpose or energize one of its accountabilities," as best as is possible with the "available resources" (Robertson 2015a, 70f.). Thus, within a role, an organizational member can make any decision that "expresses the purpose" of that role (HolacracyOne 2020, 4). In short, the organizational member has autonomy in performing the role as long as it does not violate "the domain of another role" (Robertson 2015a, 70f.) or violates any of the rules "defined in the Holacratic Constitution" (HolacracyOne 2020, 4).

The specificity of this emphasis on roles may sound surprising at first glance, because ultimately every organization relies on the differentiation of roles. However, this principle of role alignment is radicalized in holacracy by consistently assigning tasks not to individual people, but explicitly to roles. Tasks are not assigned to "Rebecca," Kim" or "Brian" in meetings, but to "Trainer," "Program Designer," or "Finance." Colleagues are addressed in meetings not as "Lee," "Rachel," or "Phoebe," but as "Marketing," "Web Manager," or "Training Manager" (Robertson 2015b, 40). "Role over Soul" is a shorthand way to sum up this principle.[15]

Merging roles creates circles, which, like roles, are defined by purposes, areas of responsibility, and tasks. Again, the central idea here is that circles are made up of roles, not people. "The circle is," according to the holacrats' credo, "not a group of people, but a group of roles." A circle, according to the Holacratic Constitution, is a "container" for organizing roles "toward a common purpose and meaning" (HolacracyOne 2020, 1.3). A circle has the autonomy "to organize itself, and to coordinate and integrate the workers of all the roles it contains" (Robertson 2015b, 45).

The starting point of a holacratic organization is the "anchor circle"—also called the general company circle—which encompasses all other circles. The overall goals of this anchor circle are identical with the overall goals of the entire organization (see Robertson 2015b, 43ff.).[16] The formation of sub-circles within this anchor circle brings together different roles that jointly fulfill a sub-goal derived from the overall purposes. These sub-circles can then be further differentiated into sub-sub-circles, which are responsible for fulfilling the sub-sub-goals derived from the sub-goals (see Robertson 2015b, 46). This differentiation into sub-circles can be repeated until the desired level of focus is achieved.

As each circle is formed, a lead link role or circle lead role, depending on the language used, is created (see Robertson 2015b, 46ff.). The lead link role is responsible for the "overall purpose" of the circle, as long as the responsibilities are not covered by other role holders in the circle (HolacracyOne 2020, 1.4). The lead link role of each circle fills

---

15 It is interesting to note that the original differentiation of "role and soul" (Robertson 2015b, 40) gradually became the principle of "role over soul" (see Peters 2018 or Robertson 2021).
16 For this provision in version 5.0 of the constitution, see HolacracyOne 2020, 1.3.3.

the roles of this circle by members, assesses their fit with regard to the role, and removes members from roles again, should they no longer fit. Which roles are to be filled is determined in the circles themselves. The only requirement is that, in addition to the lead link role filled by the parent circle, each circle also has a representative member role that represents the interests of the circle in the parent circle.

The people in the lead link roles—the lead links or circle leads—can only fill roles within their circle with a person who is also "willing to exercise them." At the same time, they must accept when people resign from these roles (HolacracyOne 2020, 1.4.1). However, if a person has taken on a role within a circle, he or she must provide the person in the lead role with information about "projects and next steps" and the "relative priority" of projects, provide "predictions" about the completion of projects, and provide information about "key performance indicators" (HolacracyOne 2020, 2.1).

Each member has an obligation to monitor the design of circles and roles for their meaningfulness, as well as the execution of the roles of other organizational members in terms of achieving their goals and fulfilling their tasks. If problems are identified in the achievement of the formulated purposes and the defined tasks, each member has the duty to address these as tensions (Laloux 2014, 120). The tensions of the members are dealt with according to a precisely defined schedule in meetings of the circle—the "Governance Meetings" and "Tactical Meetings". This is intended to facilitate both gradual improvement of the internal structure and rapid adaptation to quickly changing environmental requirements (see Robertson 2015a, 9ff.).

Changes in the formal structure are not decided by the lead link, but by all role holders within a circle according to the "consent principle," which means that, unlike the consensus principle, not all employees have to agree to a proposed solution, but no employee can have fundamental doubts about it. Any organizational member who feels that "a role should be created, changed, or eliminated" can have something put on the agenda of a "governance meeting." At the meeting, the proposer first "presents his or her proposal and the problem the proposal is intended to solve." Then anyone can ask "comprehension questions to get information or better understand the proposal," but they are not allowed to respond to the proposal themselves yet. Next, there is a "reaction round" in which everyone can react singly to the proposal, but they are not allowed to conduct a discussion. The proposer may then "further explain the intent of their proposal or modify the proposal based on the previous discussion." Next, the meeting facilitator asks participants if anyone sees a reason why "adopting this proposal could cause harm" or "set the organization back." If "there are no objections in the room"—the basic idea of the consent principle—the proposal is considered accepted. Only if someone lodges an exception is there an "open discussion" to "find a modified proposal" (see Laloux 2014, 119f.).

Don't be discouraged if you feel fatigue set in when reading the holacratic set of rules, or even just this compact summary. There may be people who enjoy reading constitutions—whether of states or of organizations—who have already spent their vacations as teenagers working through complex legal documents with a highlighter, and who use legal texts to understand the reality of the world.[17] The vast majority of people will not count themselves among this group. But to understand holacracy, you don't need to become a constitutional specialist. You understand holacracy when you look at how holacratic organizations try to avoid the effects of classical organizations.

2.1 The Thrust of Holacratic Organizations

Criticism of the classical bureaucratic organizational model essentially has three thrusts: First, *departments have to isolate* themselves from each other and therefore each department only follows its own logic. Because employees are usually only members of a department and are strongly influenced by its goals, they would have a strongly narrowed

---

17   I confess that I belonged to this group of young people who took distinct pleasure in reading constitutional texts. But I also had the impression, irritating to me at the time, that this hobby was shared by comparatively few people in my age group.

view of the organization (on this effect, see Cyert and March 1963, 164ff.). Secondly, critics emphasize that *hierarchy* leads to a loss of information and motivation. Employees further down the hierarchical pyramid would not receive the information they need to perform their tasks with the necessary care. Employees higher up would not be provided with critical information by their subordinates because of the fear of being held responsible as the bearer of bad news. Third, organizations are criticized for being in danger of suffocating from bureaucratic overregulation due to excessive *formalization*. In order to coordinate work between departments and ensure control by the hierarchy, a large number of behavioral expectations would be placed on employees, who would often not meet the requirements of the organization (see Heydebrand 1989).

Post-bureaucratic organizational concepts start at this point and promise solutions that are supposed to reduce the problems of demarcating departments from each other, to prevent the loss of information and motivation caused by hierarchy, and finally to avoid over-bureaucratization by a multitude of regulations (for examples of such attempts, see Ehrlich 1977; Semler 1995). Experiments are carried out, for example, to have employees work together in changing compositions instead of in rigid departments, to flatten hierarchies so that responsibility can be distributed among a few hierarchical levels, each of which is managed by only a few superiors with very wide management remits, and to reduce the number of formal rules by leaving it up to employees themselves in what form they want to achieve predefined or even self-imposed goals.[18]

What is the function of the characteristics of classical bureaucratic organizations, what problems do they entail, and what solutions to these problems are the representatives of the holacratic model of organization looking for?

---

18 I refrain here from classifying this triple schema in the discussion of post-bureaucratic organizations. For examples, see for the definition of post-bureaucratic organizations Heckscher 1994; Donnellon and Scullay 1994; Seabright and Delacroix 1996; Maravelias 2003; Salaman 2005; Harris, Briand, and Bellemare 2006; Kellogg, Orlikowski, and Yates 2006; McSweeney 2006; McKenna, Garcia-Lorenzo, and Bridgman 2010; Rhodes and Milani Price 2011; Heydebrand 2013.

From Departments to Circles

In the classical bureaucratic model of organization—which has prevailed in companies, administrations, police forces and hospitals since the nineteenth century at the latest—the division into departments plays a central role. Different fields of activity are formed, each of which is handled by a department—also called an area, division, segment or team, depending on its size. Employees are assigned to only one department at a time so that they can concentrate on a precisely specified task together with their colleagues in the department (see Heckscher 1994, 20). The advantage of dividing an organization into departments is that the often contradictory requirements from the environment can be processed separately in specialized departments (see also Starbuck 1988, 67). This division makes it possible to keep requirements in individual departments stable, even if others change (for example, Luhmann 1964, 306f.; Simon 1965, 63ff.). This allows the organization to make selective adjustments while stabilizing the rest.

However, the formation of departments as a central principle of organizations entails a number of unintended side-effects. The departments are, according to the critique, "responsible" but at the same time "constantly closed" (as formulated by Fuchs 1992, 20). The departments cannot "see through each other, figure each other out exactly and surely" (Luhmann 1981, 50). An assignment to one department inevitably leads to a narrowing of perspectives, because employees always focus only on the task of their own department. An understanding of the requirements of the entire organization or other departments falls largely by the wayside (see also the observation of Luhmann 1964, 308f.). In extreme cases, the work results of one department would merely be thrown over the wall to the next department and no consideration would be given to whether the latter could do anything with the work results.

The holacratic organizational model attempts to avoid these problems by replacing departments with circles. This involves much more than just the popular renaming of departments to tribes or of teams to squads. Unlike departments, circles are not assigned to people with all their organization-specific role references, but only to roles that are decoupled from people.[19] These roles are filled in the circles by people, but according to the basic holacratic understanding, people can take on different roles in different circles and also give up each of these individual roles at their own request. This is intended to eliminate a person's attachment to only one department and thus avoid the narrowing of employees' perspectives to the rationality of a single department.

Softening of the Hierarchy

Hierarchies form in organizations when the acceptance of authority to give instructions is made a condition of membership. Leadership no longer takes place on a situational basis, dependent on the competencies of individuals; instead, employees are clearly subordinated over a longer period of time to a leader who is responsible for assigning tasks (see on hierarchies as a special case of leadership Luhmann 1964, 208ff.). Hierarchies in organizations thus always simultaneously establish a relationship of inequality—namely between superiors and subordinates—and equality—namely between colleagues on the same hierarchical level (see on Luhmann 1965, 172). The hierarchical arrangement of those who give and those who receive instructions makes it possible to produce relatively unambiguous decisions relatively quickly within organizations with comparatively low negotiation costs (for a summary, see Lee and Edmondson 2017, 36). Hierarchies can greatly reduce uncertainty in organizations because superiors serve a "bottleneck" function. They filter the information from above for their employees according to its degree of relevance and at the same time condense information from below for their own superiors (Luhmann 1964, 210f.).

---

19 For relevant work on teams in post-bureaucratic organizations, see Hackman 1987; Manz and Sims 1987; Barker 1993.

But a central weakness of hierarchy lies precisely in this filtering of information through the multitude of bottlenecks inherent in a hierarchy. On the one hand, much of the information relevant for decision-making in organizations does not accrue at the top of the organization, which leads superiors to constantly complain that they are inadequately supplied with information, despite IT-supported management information systems (for just one example, see Stone 1975, 44f.). On the other hand, employees complain that they do not receive sufficient information from above to perform their tasks satisfactorily. The consequence is that "decisions are made on a distant Olympus" which are "not implementable on the ground of facts" (the complaint of Hamel 2011, which is also regularly repeated by the holacrats; here quoted from Robertson 2015b, 21). Often this results in lower motivation to perform. Members would settle down in the department, which is considered to be externally determined by the hierarchy, and in so doing would increasingly give up the claim to their own further development in the organization (for an early discussion, see McGregor 1960). The helpless reaction of superiors to this incipient inner resignation would then be to further increase the pressure (Reitzig 2022).

Holacracy does not completely abandon the hierarchical principle for structuring the organization, but it does soften it considerably in some central places. According to the holacrats—and this idea is central—there is no longer a person-bound hierarchical leadership in which superiors can give instructions to the employees assigned to them. Instead, in each circle there is only the person appointed by the superior circle to a leadership link role—the so-called lead link. This lead link role now holds the sole right to fill roles within the circle. The role assignment is not made by the lead link itself, but is determined jointly within the circle. Thus, the only formal source of power a lead link has is the ability to remove one person from a role and replace him or her with another. The effect of removing a staff member's personal assignment to a specific supervisor may be that a staff member is the lead link of a staff member in one circle and can assign or remove a role from him, but he in turn can assign or remove a role from her in another circle in which he is the lead link.

The Modification of Formalization

In the classical bureaucratic model of organization, formalization is a central mechanism for coordinating organizational members. Formalization, in complicated but precise terms in systems theory, is the linking of expectations relevant in organizations to a decision about membership. Simply put, if you want to become or remain a member of an organization, you have to do what the organization expects you to do. The effect in organizations is simple but consequential. The strikingly high level of conformity within an organization is established via the fact that membership within the organization is contingent on meeting the formal expectations of the organization (Luhmann 1964, 38). This makes it possible for relatively fixed reciprocal behavioral expectations to form in organizations, not least with regard to assignment to departments and classification in hierarchies (Luhmann 1964, 34). The result is usually a strikingly close-meshed, written network of formal expectations. This tightly meshed, codified network of formal expectations is classically referred to as bureaucracy.

But it is precisely this tightly fixed network of formal expectations that brings about a whole series of disadvantages in organizations in the form of rigidity (see the early classics of the critique of bureaucracy, especially Merton 1957; Dalton 1959; Cohen 1965; Crozier 1963). In highly formalized organizations, the criticism goes, communication would be cumbersome. Everything would have to be discussed through official channels. Because of the communication problems, there would always be duplication of work in different parts of the organization. The rules and regulations would be misused in micropolitical conflicts. Adaptation to environmental changes would take place only with a time lag. Functionless positions would not be dissolved, but would persist (for an overview of the pathologies of bureaucratic organizations, see Horch 1983, 156; Schluchter 1985, 236ff.; Rojot 2005, 48f.; Bernoux 1985, 68).

Interestingly, the principle of formalization—unlike the principles of departments and hierarchies—is not softened in the holacratic organizational model. On the contrary: every assumption of a role, every assignment to a circle, every shift of responsibility, no matter how small, is formally fixed in the organization's holacratic control software for all to see. This results in conspicuously detailed role descriptions. Here lies the central difference of the holacratic organizational model from other post-bureaucratic organizational models, in which, in addition to the softening of boundaries between departments and the reduction of hierarchy, emphasis is additionally placed on a de-formalization of expectations with the simultaneous formation of informal expectations.

Thus, the key feature of holacracy is that the hyperformalization of the organization, secured via a detailed constitution, prevents a reversion to the classical personnel-bound hierarchy and usual silo formation of departments (see Robertson 2014, 7; Lee and Edmondson 2017, 48). Friedrich Hayek argued that a constitution is a commitment that Peter enters into in a sober state in case he gets drunk (Hayek 1960, 180).[20] Similarly, a holacratic constitution can be understood as a commitment device for the head of the company, which she enters into in a calm state to prevent her from reacting hierarchically once things get restless in the organization.

2.2 The Special Form of Holacratic Formalization

While in classical organizations the change of formal structures through the reorganization of departments or the redefinition of processes is often a lengthy process, the formal structures of holacratic organizations are, at least according to the postulate, in a permanent process of change. Driven by alignment with an organization's purpose and guided by addressing tensions, rapid adjustments to the environment can be made in governance meetings. Even without decisions of a hierarchy, new circles can be constantly formed, roles newly tailored

---

20 In the original: "A constitution is a tie imposed by Peter, when sober, on Peter when drunk" (Hayek 1960, 180).

or tasks modified. Thus, a formal order would emerge that would be in a permanent state of flux (see Robertson 2015a, 9ff.).

From a systems theory perspective, what are the effects of formalization in organizations and what are the special features of holacratic formalization?

Formalization as a Generalization Service

No organization can exist without the principle of formalization. But even though at least some practitioners speak of the "need for more formality," the "change in formal structure," or the "proliferation of formality," it is often not clear what exactly they mean by formalization. To take a compact approach: Formalization can generalize expectations in organizations temporally, factually and socially (Luhmann 1964, 60). Through the generalization of expectations, according to Niklas Luhmann, individual events remain independent, are "not affected by individual deviations, breakdowns, contradictions" and even survive fluctuations "within certain limits" (Luhmann 1964, 55f.). This sounds complicated at first, but to understand organizations, it is necessary to understand the mechanism of formalization in its three manifestations.

In the *temporal dimension,* expectations in organizations can be made disappointment-proof through formalization. This is important because it is part of the everyday life of organizations that expectations are permanently disappointed: Work rules are disregarded, official channels are not followed, or targets are ignored. But formalization ensures that the question of the validity of an expectation does not arise every time it is disappointed (Luhmann 1964, 61). Organizations may violate work rules, bypass official channels, or fail to meet targets, but the formal expectations still remain. One only needs to look up the work rules, the official channels and the targets to know what is valid. Formalization makes it possible to clearly determine at any point in time whether an "expectation applies or not" (Luhmann 1964, 62).

In the *factual dimension,* formality ensures that the various roles are related to each other in a meaningful way. It would ultimately be unfavorable for an organization if different roles were not consistently related to each other in their activities. If the programmers, human resources people and salespeople were to act in their organizational roles only as they saw fit, the organization would quickly come to an end. Organizations are therefore constantly struggling to ensure that the relationships between the various roles are at least somewhat coherent. In management language, this is called competence clarification. Certainly, we know from practical experience that roles do not always mesh smoothly (a key word here is competence wrangling). But this is not necessary. For organizations it is sufficient, according to Niklas Luhmann, if the "fiction" of a meaningful connection between the roles is established (Luhmann 1964, 63). All members of an organization hold to the fiction that their roles are neatly delineated. If, however, major distortions do occur, formal decisions can be used to bring about a "clarification of roles."

In the *social dimension,* the generalization of behavioral expectations is "expressed by the fact that, within the system, consensus with the formal expectations can be assumed among all members regardless of their individually different attitudes" (Luhmann 1964, 68). This sounds complicated, but the principle is quite simple. People who want to become or remain members of the organization can be expected to accept the formal expectations of the organization. You can easily test this principle by openly saying in your organization that you are not willing to accept the formally defined requirements going forward. This would irritate not only your own superiors, colleagues and subordinates, but also other members who are not at all directly affected by your behavior. It is not a matter of fulfilling all the formal requirements of the organization in practice, but merely of participating in the "consensus fiction" that all members must adhere to the formal expectations (all these points, see Luhmann 1964: 69).

How are these general formalization mechanisms modified within the holacratic organizational model?

2.3 The Peculiarities of Holacratic Formalization

A holacratic organization is designed to constantly adapt its formal structure to the expectations of its environment. Circles and roles are formed, modified, or removed through continuous formalization. The formal structure of a holacratic system is therefore in constant flux. All changes are precisely documented in writing. According to the idea of holacracy, this documentation makes it possible to keep an organizational structure visible for all and thus to make it compatible for further changes (see Robertson 2015a, 26ff.). [21]

In the *temporal dimension,* holacratic organizations undergo a change in the way they deal with disappointments in expectations. In the classical bureaucratic variant, expectation disappointment usually evokes the response of maintaining the expectation, thus ensuring a high degree of consistency. If a work rule is violated, the official channels are ignored, or a target is not met, these formal expectations are nevertheless adhered to. In holacratic formalization, however, the disappointment of expectations—according to Phanmika Sua-Ngam-Iam's observation (2023b)—is immediately taken as a reason to question the formal structure. When there is a deviation from the formal structure, this tension is addressed in one of the holacratic meetings. Formulating this tension allows for not automatically holding on to expectations, but also allows searching for changes in the formal structure. Expressed in terms of systems theory: Instead of a normative adherence to expectations, there is a cognitive reaction to their disappointment, and the expectations themselves are questioned (Luhmann 1985, 32). The effect is a permanent change in the formal structure of the organization.

In the *factual dimension,* the holacratic approach differs from classical formalization in its pronounced attention to detail (see Sua-Ngam-Iam 2023b). Role expectations are formulated in very precise terms

---

21 I follow up here on the basic thinking of organization scholar Phanmika Sua-Ngam-Iam, who first applied the mechanisms of generalization of behavioral expectations to holacratic organizations. See Sua-Ngam-Iam and Kühl 2021.

instead of in general terms. Instead of limiting themselves to general role descriptions such as programmer, human resources manager, or salesperson, which can be interpreted situationally, these roles are spelled out in holacratic organizations down to the smallest detail. Following Chester Barnard, we can describe the process in such a way that the zones of indifference—i.e., the behaviors that the organization can expect of members without this being specified in advance—are reduced as much as possible (Barnard 1938, 168f.). In short, in the holacratic organization, all expectations are formalized to such an extent that there are, or can be, in effect no expectations that have not been cast into a formal structure.

In the *social dimension,* the distinctive feature is that organizational members are expected not only to give blanket assent to formal expectations, but to the holacratic constitution as a whole.[22] When someone becomes a member of a classical organization, they receive a rough orientation to the organization's objectives, basic structure, and roles, but it does not require the "mental anticipation of all its individual acts of execution" (Luhmann 1964, 93). Even when joining a holacratic organization, of course, not every single act of execution is defined in advance, but the members are expected to accept the elaborate holacratic set of rules. One can hardly remain a member of a holacratic organization if one rejects the basic principles of the holacratic constitution, resists taking on holacratically defined roles, or does not participate in the holacratic interaction formats.[23] One must at least pretend to follow the principles set forth in the constitution.

---

22 At this point, I depart from the argument of Phanmika Sua-Ngam-Iam, who locates the specificity of holacratic formalization in the attempt to blur participation and performance motivation. In holacracy, she argues, consensus can be assumed not only on the general formal structure, but also on the specific formal structure, since members can help shape the formal structure whenever it is changed. Members could therefore shape the formal structure themselves, to which they then submit, and therefore agree with each change not only to a general, but also to this specific formal structure.

23 This is the reason why quite a few members leave an organization during the transition to holacracy. This separation process is supported by holacratic organizations (on Zappos, see Anders 2014; Groth 2015a; Groth 2015b; Groth 2016; Kumar and Mukherjee 2018; Reingold 2016. For the introduction of holacracy at Zappos, see also the biography of Tony Hsieh by Grind and Sayre 2022, 101ff.

2.4 The Bureaucratization of Post-Bureaucratic Organizations

Holacracy is ultimately the hyperformalized version of a management concept that has been known for decades and has largely been forgotten for a while: sociocracy. Holacracy borrowed from sociocracy the idea of the circles, which are meant to form their own goals and control goal achievement themselves. The holacratic idea of connecting subordinate circles with the superordinate circles through lead and representation members was copied from sociocracy.[24] The idea that decisions are made under the "consent principle," which means that suggestions are considered as accepted if no serious objections are brought forward, existed already in sociocracy.[25] In the early days, the holacrats explicitly identified the sociocratic roots of holacracy.[26] With the increasing commercialization of holacracy, however, these clear references to sociocratic roots blurred beyond recognition.[27]

Despite its hyperformalization, holacracy is often portrayed as a measure to prevent the effects of bureaucratization. Those who implement holacracy describe their mission as "busting bureaucracy" (see Groth 2018b, 73). According to the holacrats, their mission is to "kill bureaucracy" in order to survive in the Darwinian struggle for corporate survival (see Groth 2018b, 91).[28] The paradoxical result of this anti-

---

24 Sociocracy had copied the idea that not only the superior circle sends a representative to the subordinate one, but also the subordinate circles are represented in the superior one by an elected representative, from Rensis Likert (see Likert 1967; see also Likert 1961 and later Likert and Araki 1986). The standard text of holacracy no longer references Likert (see in addition Robertson 2015b).
25 For examples of sociocracy, see Endenburg 1988; Endenburg and Bowden 1988; Zeleny 1989.
26 For example, see Wittrock 2007, 5f. or also Robertson 2014, 6. An earlier variant of holacracy by Robertson still stated, "Sociocracy provided a large part of the answer we were searching for" (Robertson 2006: 5).
27 In the standard work of the holacrats, there is only a brief mention of sociocratic roots—hidden in an acknowledgement (Robertson 2015a, 174).
28 In a conversation with Tony Hsieh, then CEO of Zappos, he had the following to say in this context: "Darwin said that the species that survive are not the strongest or most intelligent, but the most adaptable to change," he said, looking out into the crowd. "I believe the same is true with companies. We must adapt, or we'll die." He cited the fact that most Fortune 500 companies from the last half century are no longer around today. The way to prevent that from happening with Zappos, he said, is to kill bureaucracy and develop a new system for doing things (Groth 2018b, 91).

bureaucratic movement, however, is its conspicuous bureaucratization in the face of the hyperformalization of the organization described above. Every expectation of an organizational member, no matter how small, is set down in detail in writing, every relationship between the individual roles in the organization is precisely defined, every decision-making process is set down in a detailed file.

Even if we are reluctant to use the term "office" in modern management, this inevitably reminds us of Max Weber's principles of bureaucracy. In holacracy, as in the "bureaucratic administrative staff" described by Weber, the focus is on a "continuous, rule-bound operation of official business" (Weber 1976, 125). The organization member is integrated with "fixed official competences," into a "fixed official hierarchy" and—abstracting from personal views and resentments—is supposed to orientate himself towards the "factual official duties" (Weber 1976, 126). Even more consequently than in Weber's conception of bureaucracy, the principle of the "file dependency of administration" is implemented in holacracy, in which "oral discussions" are controlled via holacratic software and every decision, no matter how small, is "fixed in writing" (Weber 1976, 126).[29]

It is particularly striking that these bureaucratization effects already begin with holacracy in micro-organizations. It is remarkable that holacracy is predominantly practiced by micro-organizations. Sometimes these have one or two dozen employees, but sometimes only two or three (for a first rough analysis, see Zeuch 2016a). The high proportion of holacratic micro-organizations is particularly striking because in research it is assumed that micro-organizations in most cases want to do without formalization—and thus bureaucratization—and are often able to do so. This is because micro-organizations function as face-to-face organizations in which all organizational members know each other and conduct internal voting together around a conference

---

29 On Weber's theory of bureaucracy, see also Selznick 1943; Blau 1954; Constas 1958; Eisenstadt 1958; Eisenstadt 1959; Udy 1959; Stinchcombe 1959; Presthus 1961; Hall 1962; Hilbert 1987; Adler 1999. For a relevant monograph, see Gouldner 1954; Blau 1954; Blau and Meyer 1971. On the relation of the conception of post-bureaucracy to Weber's theory of bureaucracy, see Höpfl 2006.

table. However, one reason for the high proportion of micro-organizations among holacratic organizations could be that only organizations with a small number of employees are even capable of handling the high formal requirements of holacracy. With growth in personnel, the formal regulations within the organizations increase, so that at some point they can no longer be processed by the holacratic organization.

When the word "bureaucracy" is used by organizational practitioners, it often has a negative connotation. Bureaucracy sounds like inflexibility, ossification, rule fetishism. Organizational scientists take a different stance on bureaucratization effects. They recognize the function of bureaucratization effects as an objectification of the approach in organizations and recognize their central importance for the emergence of the organization (see classically Weber 1976, 561f.). Thus, when organization scholars emphasize the bureaucratization of holacratic organizations because of their hyperformalization, this is not meant as a criticism. What is striking, with a distanced view, is merely the paradoxical effect that under the banner of bureaucracy critique there is an intensified bureaucratization of post-bureaucratic organizations.

3.
The Renaissance of the Purposive-Rational Organizational Model

> "You are responsible for recording and tracking all projects and next actions for your role in a database or comparable, concrete manner. This includes regularly reviewing and updating this database so that it reflects a reliable listing of the role's active and potential work."
> *Call to role holders in version 4.1. of the holacratic constitution*
> (HolacracyOne 2015, 9)

Holacrats describe their organizational model as a fundamentally new, comprehensive "operating system" for organizations (Robertson 2015a, 14f.).[30] Holacracy, they say, is not a classical Utilities Control Room or software, but a "social technology." Just as a computer would have an operating system, organizations should have such an operating system that "controls how communication happens, how power works, how applications share resources and information, and how the flow of work" is managed (Robertson 2012; quoted from Laloux 2014, 118f.).

Even before holacracy, according to the holacrats, there would have been an operating system in every organization. However, this had often not been consciously planned and had often not been questioned at all. This model, based on hierarchy and silo formation, would have had a "kind of monopoly on the market of operating systems for organizations." Of course, there would have been "some variations," but ulti-

---

30 Literally, the original states, "After many years of experimentation, across several organizations, a comprehensive new operating system emerged, through my efforts and those of many others" (Robertson 2015a, 16). The term operating system is used frequently by Brian Robertson in his book. On the use of the term in the reception of the management concept, see also, for example Groth 2013; Denning 2014; Mont 2017.

mately they would always have been based on the same power structures and ways of working (Robertson 2012; quoted in Laloux 2014, 119).

To truly transform organizations, the holacrats argue, change could no longer simply be "bolting" onto the existing standard operating system. Instead, they argue, the organization's traditional "operating system," based on personal hierarchy and departmentalization, must be "upgraded" to a "new operating system" (Robertson 2015a, 15). The necessary cuts are, according to the metaphor, similar to the changeover of computers from the MS-DOS operating system to Windows. When people were still working with the old Microsoft operating system with its "black screen with clunky green text," it was hard to imagine that it would be replaced by "an interactive, user-friendly, graphical interface" that "updates itself" and is "constantly connected to a worldwide virtual network" (Robertson 2015a, 15).

The software metaphor suggests that it is a matter of developing a system that defines the basic rules of interaction between individual components. An operating system does not determine which concrete programs are based on it, but it has a decisive influence on their processes. But if it does not succeed in developing a functioning operating system, all programs function—so the implication—slowly, unstably and in a manner prone to error (according to Mitterer 2015). In this way, holacracy purports to be an operating system in which all elements mesh neatly and a multitude of other programs can be placed on top of it.

The metaphor of the operating system sounds plausible at first. Like many metaphors used to describe organizations, it seems convincing precisely because of its simplicity. But what kind of organizational understanding lies behind this concept of a self-controlling operating system?

3.1 The Notion of Purposive-Rational Planning of the Organization

Many advocates of new forms of organization see a meaningful orientation of the organization as the starting point. This sets the tenor for creating a soulful organization in which a longing for a radically different way of working together in organizations can find its place (Laloux 2014, 4).

Here, as with many management concepts, this cultivates the dream of organizations as "places" in which people create meaning every day through what they do. "People," the idea goes, go to work "with joy," meet each other there "as human beings," and "unfold their potential." At the end of the day, people go home at least as "energized and fulfilled as they had appeared at work" (Fink and Moeller 2018, 1f.).

The idea is that organizations doing these things would not only contribute "to their own lives and well-being" but equally to that of their customers, business partners, and capital providers. Ultimately, this would trigger processes in these organizations that would protect the environment and preserve natural foundations, resulting in a "positive development of the social environment" (Fink and Moeller 2018, 1f.).

While such dreams have long been a prerogative of self-managed enterprises, grassroots political initiatives, and utopian living communities (see Paranque and Willmott 2014), they have now entered the mainstream of management. Despite all the problems with exhaust gas manipulation, environmental pollution or corruption, even large companies in the automotive, pharmaceutical and energy industries now believe that the solution to the problem of employee motivation lies in finding a higher purpose for their undertakings. Every organization, so the assumption goes, has "its own purpose," "its own telos," which must be worked out by the "top circle" (Robertson 2006, 17).

The buzzword for this constellation of ideas is the "purpose-driven organization." By formulating a purpose, organizations "open up a large umbrella" under which "the most diverse people with their talents, intentions, and experiences can unite" to pursue a common goal. In fact, purpose is "far more than a goal." It is the "reason why we get up in the morning and go to work," "why we make an effort, get involved, and take risks" (a pathos common in management discourse; see Linke 2016).

Consistently, underdetermined superlatives dominate the formulations of the purpose of holacratic organizations (see Strothotte 2023). Purpose descriptions teem with terms like "awesome," "cutting edge," "exquisite," or "transformative," intended to describe the "creative potential" of the "living system" (according to Robertson in Laloux 2014, 200).

But we must not jump to conclusions about the concrete functioning of holacratic organizations on the basis of ethereal purpose formulations. A classic mistake in the analysis of organizations is not to distinguish systematically between value and goals formulations (see Luhmann 1973, 33ff.). Purposes are abstract value formulations that provide only a rough frame of reference; they do not determine what is right or wrong behavior. Goals, on the other hand, are programs that define what is to be achieved at a certain point in time and whether its achievement or non-achievement can be determined.

One mistake in analyzing organizations is to naively assume that goals can be derived from the values of the organization. Yet values and goals serve quite different functions in the organization. *Values* serve more to decorate the display side and at best provide rough orientation frameworks, while setting *goals* enables the organization to be controlled. At best, the values and goals of an organization are loosely coupled.

Beyond the usual rhetoric surrounding purpose, how do holacrats envision structuring organizations?

The Breakdown of the Original Goal

In the beginning, according to the holacrats, each organization has a kind of original goal. This original goal is determined by the leadership of a holacratic organization in the anchor circle, or in the general company circle. Starting from this original goal, the whole holacratic organization is then constructed in the form of ends-means chains. Working from the original goal, a multitude of means are derived in the form of sub-goals and sub-sub-goals. These sub-goals and sub-sub-goals then serve as functions for circles and then for roles.

In practice, when a holacratic constitution is adopted, organizations are not re-planned on the drawing board from top to bottom. Rather, the goals statements that have guided the work in the individual units to date serve as the starting point. In this, the holacrats follow the tradition of Frederick Taylor in that the starting point of a more rational organizational design is the individual tasks to be accomplished in an organization.[31] In the end, the tasks should then be interrelated in such a way that there is a consistent arrangement from the very top to the very bottom.

Here we can recognize the idea, which was already present in Max Weber, that organizations can be understood as rational arrangements of ends and means. According to Weber's well-known formulation, people act in purposive-rational ways (1976, 13) when they assess different goals in choosing actions, choose the most favorable means to achieve the defined goals, and takes into account possible undesirable side effects in this selection process of ends and means.

The Nesting of Goals and Circles

The determination of goals, sub-goals and sub-sub-goals is coordinated in the holacratic organizational model in nested circles, sub-circles and sub-sub-circles. The starting point is always the comprehensive circle—the anchor circle or general company circle—through which the goal of the organization is defined. Starting from this upper circle, sub-circles are set up which are responsible for achieving the sub-goals derived from the upper goal.

This breaks with the classical hierarchical structure in that the superior circle can occupy the lead link of the subordinate circle, but the exact determination of the sub-goal is left to the responsible circle itself and the fulfillment of the tasks is monitored by the subordinate circle itself.

---

31 Taylor must be understood here in distinction to Harrington Emerson (1924), who sought to derive functions from the overall goals of the organization. For the controversy between the contemporaries Taylor and Emerson, see Witzel 2012, 186ff.

The superordinate circle can only address tensions if task determination is not aligned with the superordinate goal or if the determined task is not achieved. Although the holacratic organizational model does not represent a classical hierarchical order, it is striking how strongly the structure of upper, lower, and subordinate circles correlates with the hierarchical order of ends and means (see the insights in Luhmann 1973, 73).

The Selection of Suitable Personnel

As soon as the circles and roles necessary for the fulfillment of the task have been determined from the goal of the organization, they should be filled by suitable staff according to the holacratic understanding of organization. The selection of people for a role within a circle is the responsibility of the respective lead link. In doing so, it is important—and in this respect the idea does not differ from Frederick Taylor's basic consideration—to identify the most suitable people for a role.

It is important to note that according to this holacratic understanding of organization, a role with corresponding tasks must always be defined in the first step, and only in the second step is a suitable person selected for this role. In organizational science, this is referred to as the "ad-rem principle." From this perspective, tailoring jobs to a person who has already been hired—the "ad personam" principle—can only be understood as a pathology that is conceivable in exceptional cases at best. According to this logic, the choice of staff should always be based on the tasks, not the other way around (see Luhmann 1971, 209).

3.2 The Hope of Hyperformalization of the Organization

From a systems theory perspective, three sides of organizations can be distinguished. With the display side, an organization presents itself to the outside world in an embellished form. The front of the organization may contain elements of the formal side of the organization, but consists to a considerable extent of general value formulations that make the organization appear attractive in its environment. However, because of the abstract nature of such pronouncements, these general value statements serve—if at all—only as rough points of orientation for the members. The formal side of organizations is the written set of rules and the official requirements that members must follow or fulfill—at least in their presentation to other members—if they want to remain members of the organization. However, because only part of the expectations in organizations can be regulated via the formal side, an informal—or cultural—side almost inevitably develops at the same time. This involves not only typical organizational ways of thinking and forms of perception, but also, and especially, expectations of action that are not aligned with the formal requirements of the organization, or may even contradict them.

The Correspondence of the Three Sides of the Organization

Holacracy claims to have found a management concept with which these three sides of the organization can be reconciled (see Sua-Ngam-Iam 2023b).[32] Although the formal side defines membership conditions within an organization, most people, according to the holacrats, had no idea what the "formal structure" relevant to them even consisted of. Most employees, they said, did not know where to find their "job description," let alone exactly what was in them. These job descriptions, the holacrats observed, are already "out of date" by the time "they come out of the printer." Much more important for their work, they say, is what the holacrats, following Elliott Jaques (1989), identify as the "actual structure" that regulates "who makes which decisions or who

---

32 Tony Hsieh, former CEO of Zappos, noted that there are different organizational charts in companies. There is the one that exists on paper, the one that the company functions according to "in reality," and then there is the one that the company wants to have in order to function as efficiently as possible. The goal of holacracy, he said, is to bring these organizational charts as close together as possible. See also Groth 2013.

is responsible for which projects." The goal of holacracy is to merge this "formal structure" and the "extant structure" into an "essential structure" that is "most natural for the work and purpose of the organization" (Robertson 2015b, 34f.).[33]

If tensions develop in the informal space of an organization, these would have to be addressed in the designated meetings, and formal rules would have to be found that can reduce these tensions. If organizational members are bothered by short service routes, creative workarounds or useful illegalities, these would have to be replaced by formal rules that everyone can live with. In this understanding of organization, the prevailing informal structures ultimately serve only as an occasion to create better formal structures.

The hope is that the permanent optimization made possible in this way will make it unnecessary for the organization to make itself look good by means of a display side that is decoupled from the formal order. Because the formal structure is permanently improved, it can, according to this idea, also be used for external presentation, because, via the organizational control software, all members have access to the roles and tasks of all colleagues, to all problems discussed in all circles and to all decisions made; however, these are also made accessible to non-members to a large extent at the same time.[34]

The goal of permanent adaptation to the "essential structure" is to restore the "formal structure" to its deserved validity. "Employees in a holacratic organization" should refer to their own job descriptions and those of their colleagues "regularly, sometimes daily." If the "job descriptions contain relevant, accurate, clear, and useful information about what can usefully be done and what can be expected," they

---

33 The references to Elliott Jaques by the holacrats are interesting because as a psychoanalyst he originally developed strong interests in the culture of the organization. See his first book, Jaques 1951.
34 The websites of consulting firms that introduce the holacratic organizational model for their clients are quite illustrative in this regard. On these websites, role assignments, function descriptions, and decision-making processes are completely visible even to non-members. Here, in each profile, you can not only see the job description of each individual employee by clicking on "see my roles in Glassfrog," but you also have access to the decision-making processes of each circle.

would regain their original function as a central point of reference. In this way, it is possible for "how we really work" to be aligned with "what is in writing" and more closely aligned with what is best for the organization. The "actual structure," the "formal structure," and the "essential structure" would be consistently aligned (Robertson 2015b, 36f.).

Ignoring the Organizational Culture

This perspective explains why organizational culture does not play a role in the representations of holacracy proponents (see Hasenzagl and Müller 2020, 16). The original idea behind the concept of organizational culture was that the success of organizations depends on both their formal structures and the informal structure of their organizational culture. The holacrats break away from this idea, which dominated the discussion of post-bureaucratic organizational models for a long time, with their claim that all informal goals, roles and tasks should also be formally represented in the organizational control software.

The result of this attitude toward organizational culture in the holacratic approach is the hyperformalization of the organization described above. Instead of giving the informal play of organizational culture some room to breathe, every decision is recorded in the holacratic software and can be viewed by everyone, every assumption of responsibility is fixed in a role, all tasks are written down, and all discussion processes are recorded in electronic files.[35]

---

35 In this variant, the holacratic organizational model strongly resembles the Harzburg model, which dominated the German-speaking world for fifty years (for a comprehensive discussion of the Harzburg model, see Höhn 1969 and Höhn 1978; critically Guserl 1973). What in the Harzburg model was the "General Management Instruction" is in the holacratic concept the "Constitution" (*Verfassung*). In the length of job descriptions for individual employees, the holacratic model hardly differs from the Harzburg model. The striking structural similarities between Harzburg and holacracy have not yet been analyzed in detail and are not even recognized in a large part of the texts about holacracy.

3.3 A More Sophisticated Variant of the Machine Model of the Organization

With its emphasis on constant optimization of the formal structure, the holacratic organizational model is ultimately a sophisticated variant of the machine model of organization (see, for example, Hasenzagl 2020, 185).[36] Max Weber already pointed out that bureaucracy was characterized by a "technical superiority over any other form." With its "precision, speed, unambiguity, file knowledge, continuity, discretion, uniformity, tight subordination, savings in friction," bureaucracy would function like a perfected organizational machine that had nothing to do with the earlier forms of organization more reminiscent of the "mechanical modes of producing goods" (Weber 1976, 561f.).

The machine model assumes that an organization consists of precisely defined individual parts that stand in precisely defined relationships to one another. Here, all individual parts are aligned with the goal of the organization and only become meaningful in interaction with the other parts. An organization, like a machine, may consist of a great many individual parts and links, but ultimately its complexity is manageable through precise descriptions of processes. Through careful intervention, individual parts and their relationships can be changed, thus aligning the organization with new requirements. The organization manual—in effect a kind of instruction manual—merely becomes thicker as a result (for an informative discussion of the machine model of organization, see Morgan 1980, 613f.).

Compared to the classic machine model of the organization, which relies heavily on the top-down determination of the interaction of the individual parts, the holacratic organizational model determines the interaction of the individual parts more from below. In the case of very stable basic principles—the holacratic rules laid down in the constitution—the concrete interaction of the individual parts can be

---

36 Following Hasenzagl (2019), it would be interesting to ask how the "mechanistic" and "humanistic" ideologies of new forms of organization are combined in the holacratic model of organization. For this purpose, a further elaboration on the making of this management concept is planned.

optimized more easily and also adapted more quickly to changing conditions. The holacratic organization manual is at least as thick as that of the classical machine model of the organization, yet it can be rewritten more easily in many places.

4.
Unintended Side Effects of the Bureaucratization of Post-Bureaucratic Organizations

"Holacracy feels like playing a game of Management Dungeons & Dragons. Models like holacracy were created by people who tend to enjoy complex processes."

Bud Caddell (2016) on his experience implementing holacracy

The dream of the optimal organizational structure has existed as long as there have been organizations. Despite all attempts to differentiate them from the classic forms of organization based on the division of labor and hierarchy, even the promoters of new forms of organization maintain that there are organizational models that enable optimal adaptation to the demands of the environment. When proponents of the holacratic organizational model promise considerable improvements in efficiency, innovation and motivation, they are ultimately only propagating a new version of the best possible form of organization.

In this respect, the propagation of holacratic organizations is aligned with the tradition of the contingency approach in organizational research (classical Burns and Stalker 1961; Lawrence and Lorsch 1967; Donaldson 2001). The specificity of the contingency approach is that, as in Taylorism, a "one best way" of organization is assumed, but this is seen as dependent on an organization's environmental situation. While in a stable environment it is assumed that an organization built on clearly delineated departments, steep hierarchies and formal regulations is best, for volatile environments an organizational form is advocated that has less silo formation, flatter hierarchies and reduced formality.

Research on classical forms of organization has already focused on the unintended side-effects of strong formalization (see Selznick 1949;

Merton 1957; Crozier 1963). After the advantages of bureaucratic organizations were first elaborated in the tradition of Weber (see Udy 1959), the focus shifted more and more to the disadvantages of these organizational forms (see also Blau 1956). In addition to the unintended effects of formalization, scholars concentrated particularly on the ramifications of hierarchy and the formation of departments (see for example Thompson 1961).

For the analysis of holacratic organizations, we have to turn this perspective on its head, insofar as holacratic models drive formalization from below in an attempt to prevent the formation of person-based hierarchies and the differentiation of departments. The unintended side effects of the holacratic form of organization therefore have similarities to those of classic bureaucratic organizations, but they develop in specific ways.[37]

4.1 The Pull of Formalization

The holacratic model of organization claims that the formal structure is continuously better and better adapted to the expectations brought to the organization. In order to fulfill these expectations, according to the holacrats, it is necessary to always create new circles, roles or tasks and to abolish them again when they are no longer necessary to fulfill an goal. If this assumption is correct, this should create a permanent flow of establishment and abolition of circles, roles and tasks in holacratic organizations.

The effect, however, is often different. In holacratic organizations, new circles, roles or tasks are created all the time, but their abolition is rather the exception. Thus, in the control software of holacratic companies, even if the number of employees remains the same, the num-

---

37 The paradoxes of introducing holacratic forms of organization cannot be addressed. On this point, see the insights of Schell and Bischof 2022, 126ff. As a contrast, see the well-studied paradoxes in the introduction of low-formalized post-bureaucratic forms in Kühl 2020a, 27ff.

ber of circles continues to increase, the roles become more and more differentiated, and the set of rules becomes more and more detailed.[38] There seems to be a tendency inherent in holacracy toward ever greater formalization.

The pull of formalization in holacratic organizations is particularly evident in the organization of particularly sensitive issues, such as hiring, compensation, and firing. These issues are not regulated by the holacratic constitution, but one can see the extent to which holacratic organizations resort to elaborate formal procedures to resolve these issues, which are often emotionally charged in organizations. Complex systems of badges are created with which employees can prove their qualifications and experience. These must then be verified in an elaborate process by roles or circles created for this goal before they can then serve as the basis for negotiating a salary increase (on the effects, see for example Groth 2018b, 161; see also Carr 2015b).

The Formation of Formality Ruins

One effect of increasing formal regulation is the formation of formality ruins. Circles are set up that almost never meet for tactical meetings or governance meetings. Organizational members are assigned to the newly created roles, but in fact they do not function in these roles. Tasks become more and more differentiated without reflecting the activities in the respective roles. Formal expectations seem to be formulated again and again in the holacratic governance software, but in fact they have no meaning for the organization.

The organization often doesn't notice these ruins of formality until a new organizational member takes the holacratic principle seriously and contacts a designated role with a concern. Sometimes it is only then that someone notices that, due to the departure of a staff member, this role has not been filled by a person for months or years. No

---

38 This still lacks quantitative studies that use holacratic software to examine how the number of circles, roles, domains, and accountabilities have changed over several years.

one has noticed the non-occupation of this role because it had no real significance in the day-to-day work of the organization, but no one has seen the need to abolish this role.[39]

The Paradoxical Effects of Downsizing Campaigns

Holacratic organizations react to the proliferation of their formal structures with streamlining campaigns. There are calls to review whether the circles that have been created still make sense, and there are discussions about their abolition. Organizational members with more than twenty roles are asked to reduce the number. An appeal is made to the role holders to ensure that the function descriptions of the roles are still appropriate.

But it is one of the paradoxes of hyperformalized organizations that these measures result in a further push toward formalization. Separate roles are created that are supposed to act as "garbage collectors" to ensure that roles that have become unnecessary are removed. Separate formal programs are created to ensure that the circles are purged.

Holacracy suffers an effect of formalization that has been well studied for classical bureaucratic organizations.[40] In most cases, the response to problems in the organization is to create new formal structures, in the form of new communication channels or new programs or the hiring of new staff. De-bureaucratization campaigns, regularly proclaimed in the face of the proliferation of formalization, then lead to new formal regulations, the creation of new positions, and the hiring of new personnel (see Luhmann 2018, 283).[41]

---

39 We have noticed the ruins of formality in our empirical studies, especially in larger holacratic organizations. They can also be observed from the outside in smaller holacratic organizations, which allow external access to their holacratic control software via the website. It is conspicuously common to find circles there that show no activity for months.
40 Holacracy requires, according to the CEO of a company that has ditched holacracy, a "deep passion for record keeping" (cited in Carr 2016). The original English blog post by Ev Williams states "Holacracy also requires a deep commitment to recordkeeping and governance" (see Carr 2016).
41 One can observe the proliferation of formal structure already at the level of the "operating system" itself—the holacratic constitution. While it was initially presented as a "general

Organizational concepts that rely on hyperformalization resemble a soccer game in which the behavioral expectations for players are specified in ever more detail in a set of written rules. The team's "goal"—winning a game—is translated into increasingly detailed written rules specifying that soccer players should strive to win the ball, pass it only to their own teammates, and ultimately kick it into the opponent's goal. Each lost game will then be taken as an opportunity to specify the formal requirements even further, specifying to whom the balls should be passed, whether they should be passed high or flat, and when which fouls should be committed. In the end, the soccer team can be handed a rulebook of thousands of pages detailing how to proceed (for this metaphor, see Dollase 2011, 9).

4.2 Withdrawal Possibilities Through a Variety of Roles

Holacracy promises to tackle the problem of motivating organizational members. Classical organizations have to grapple with the fact that pressure may be the only method to make members do their job decently. Due to the lack of identification with the organization, members would repeatedly try to evade expectations despite the pressure. In the worst case, "internal resignations" would occur, in which people would remain members of the organization but would in effect behave like non-members (for more on this phenomenon, see Höhn 1986).

Holacrats argue that the motivation problem does not arise in their organizations because the members, who identify with the purpo of the organization, could choose their own roles and design them according to their demands. In holacracy, employees are no longer be forced to take on pre-scripted roles; instead, they can pick and choose and

---

system with a minimal number of practices" (Laloux 2015, 119); the number of rules in the holacratic constitution has continued to grow. While there have been repeated attempts to reduce the number of words and sentences and average sentence lengths, the holacratic constitution remains a complex set of rules, even for experts (see HolacracyOne 2020).

design their roles within the member role. If members in a holacratic organization are no longer satisfied with their roles, the management concept allows them to hand over this role and look for a new one.

The Supposed Solution to the Problem of Indeterminacy in Employment Contracts

In organizations, it is not possible to describe the activities of an organizational member down to the smallest detail as soon as he or she joins. In every organization, there are inevitably tasks that have not yet been specified when the member joins, rules that have not yet been made known in detail at the start date, or decision-making paths that have not been made explicit at the beginning. Even if such specifications are comparatively precise for jobs on the assembly line, in the call center, or in logistics, the organization cannot guarantee that these requirements will remain stable over a longer period of time. Thus, employment contracts can never specify exactly what the organization member can expect in detail (on this feature of contracts in general, see Hart 2009, 24ff.).

This indeterminate quality of work contracts provides organizational members with an opportunity to escape work demands. This problem has been described from various theoretical perspectives. Marxist thought maintains that the purchase of labor power by the capitalist is not equivalent to the real use of labor power by capital (Marx 1962, p. 532ff.), and that the capitalist's fantasies are directed to how he can solve this *problem of transformation of* purchased labor power into factual labor power (on this, see Braverman 1974, 41ff.). In systems theory, the transformation problem is referred to as the fundamental *difference between membership and participation motivation of* organizational members (on this, see Luhmann 1979, 199). In principal-agent theory, this phenomenon is described as *shirking*. Agents, in this case workers, are bought in to perform certain services for a principal, the entrepreneur, and tend, out of their own utility orientation, to want to achieve the principal's rewards by performing as little as possible (see an early discussion in Jones 1984; Moe 1984; for an application to holacracy, see Sua-Ngam-Iam 2023b).

Research has shown that management cannot fundamentally eliminate the transformation problem through new concepts (see Edwards 1979; Littler 1982; compact overviews in, e.g. Littler and Salaman 1982; Littler 1990; Kühl 2019b). In capitalism, people take on jobs not primarily because they see meaning in them, but because they are forced to sell their labor power for their everyday survival (arguing along the lines of Spencer 2000; Smith 2015).

Even the infusion of an organization with a "purpose" does not change the fact that the members of the organization have to earn money in order to finance their lives. The problem of a difference between membership and participation motivation thus arises in holacratic organizations in a similar form as in classical organizations, but is addressed differently.

Effects of Abandoning Hierarchical Assignments

Classical bureaucratic organizations, with their clearly hierarchical assignment of employees, deal with the transformation problem by having superiors ensure, as part of their monitoring and control function, that employees work in accordance with the tasks assigned to them. It is part of the job description of superiors to ensure that their employees actually perform as expected of them, to confront them if they fail to do so, and to ensure their removal from the organization if necessary.

In contrast, most post-bureaucratic organizations operating with fixed self-directing teams solve the transformation problem by having team members ensure, via direct feedback, that no one can shirk. Perceived performance holdbacks thus became personal problems between the peer members of a team (for examples of the pressure in teams that often results from this, see Kühl 2017, 81ff.; see on teams in post-bureaucratic organizations also Manz and Sims 1984; Manz and Sims 1987; Langfred 2000).

It is precisely these bureaucratic and post-bureaucratic mechanisms for ensuring service delivery that are complicated in holacratic organizations by the assumption of roles in various circles (see Schell and Bischof 2022, 130).[42] Organizational members may point out that they cannot perform as expected in their roles in one circle just now because they are particularly challenged in their roles in another circle at the moment. Because holacratic organizations—at least in terms of the idea—dispense with the hierarchical assignment of members, there is no body that addresses this problem. Because the system rejects staff hierarchy, there is hardly another form of organization in which employees can hide so easily by assuming a multitude of roles.

Again, holacratic organizations seek resolution through formalized procedures (see Cowan 2017). For example, each role in a holacratic organization is assigned a certain number of points. Employees who do not accumulate enough points in their respective roles are then not immediately dismissed, but moved to a zone from which they can try to take on roles with sufficient points. If they fail to accumulate roles with sufficient points in a designated period of time, they are fired by the role owners responsible for this process in the system (for the variant at Zappos, see Carr 2015b; see also Groth 2018b, 206; 218).[43]

4.3. The Reduction of Initiatives Beyond the Formal Structure

The holacratic organizational model is designed to allow each organizational member to take their own initiatives.[44] Holacracy, according to its proponents, was "designed" to harness and honor the "uniquely

---

[42] The central element of holacracy is the separation of roles and people. The goal of the holacratic organization is to achieve its purpose with the help of the roles required for this purpose, independently of the people who hold these roles. Only after the necessary roles have been identified can the search be conducted for the people with the right fit. This often leads to people taking on multiple roles (see Robertson 2015a, 38).
[43] On the adoption of holacracy at Zappos, see also an early analysis by Yugendhar and Ali 2017. On the difficulties of transition, see also Josserand, Teo, and Clegg 2006.
[44] See also the principle of "Getting Things Done" by David Allen (2001), which plays an important role in holacracy.

human capacity" of creativity and to create a space for initiatives from each organizational member. The result for each individual in a "holacracy-powered" organization, they say, is the "deeply fulfilling experience" of being a "creative partner" rather than merely a "cog in the system" (Robertson 2017).[45]

Holacracy also enables members to take initiatives that violate the formal structure if a member has a reasonable belief that the delay incurred by seeking authorization would result in a reduction of the action's potential impact. This "action outside the formal structure" refers only to a single decision. As soon as decisions become structural in nature, the holacrats believe that this must take place by changing the formal structure in a governance process (see Robertson 2015a, 34).

The Legitimization of Initiatives Through a Role

When acting independently, one point is important to holacrats. Initiatives are limited by the roles specified by holacracy. In this context, each member has the right to make decisions in his or her role as long as no competing priorities have been established by the formal structure and the area of responsibility of another role is not affected (see Robertson 2015a, 37). In short, there is considerable scope for decision-making, but only if a member is assigned a role to do so.

There are good reasons for this limitation to role-appropriate behavior. Sven Kette observes that organizations "love" predictability. The "great achievement of formalization" is that "communication becomes expectable." Defining roles, describing tasks, specifying responsibilities, establishing circles, determining who is responsible, and establishing rules of conversation ensures that the organization is not caught off guard. Initiatives then "always represent an attack—at least an implicit one—on the formal structure" (according to Kette 2021, 132f.).

---

45 Literally, "Holacracy is designed specifically to harness and honor this uniquely human capacity" and "The result, for each human being in a holacracy-powered organization, is a much more deeply fulfilling experience of being a creative partner rather than a cog in the system" (see Robertson 2017).

This also applies to activities that go beyond the role in hyperformalized organizations. However, there is an attempt to discipline the role by fitting it into a well-defined formal form. If someone wants to make a difference in a holacratic organization, then they must have their existing role set expanded or have a new role created. In doing so, changes must be legitimized through the integration of other organizational members in the affected circles. Debates about change are thus civilized through formalized meetings specified in detail. This is planned change in its ideal form.

The Effects of Formalizing Initiatives

This approach means that the process for launching overarching change is extremely costly. When an organization runs under holacracy, a common criticism goes, you would no longer simply ask your colleague Elizabeth to develop a new collaboration tool; instead, you would first define a role, create a purpose, a domain, and a list of accountabilities, initiate a steering meeting to activate that new role, and then delegate the initiative to develop that new tool to that role. Holacracy, skeptics argue, would "empower" roles, not people—and that's exactly the problem (Appelo 2016).[46]

When people take initiatives that go beyond these formal specifications to make a change, they take a risk. The initiatives are understood as a critique of the carefully crafted formal structure. In hyperformalized organizations, therefore, people who take initiatives that are not backed up by the formal structure almost inevitably encounter resistance. They are considered "agitators" who are unsettling the organization with their "strange ideas," or "troublemakers" who do not appreciate the stability of the formal structure (see Kette 2021, 126). Initiators are thwarted by referring to the change procedures as long as it takes for them to get in line or leave the organization. There is

---

46 Literally, "After all, holacracy doesn't authorize human beings; it authorizes roles. Or, in other words, holacracy does not empower people, it empowers processes" (Appelo 2016).

no place for "pattern breakers," "organizational rebels" or "corporate revolutionaries" in hyperformalized organizations.

Ultimately, the criticism goes, a holacratic organization could become ossified. "More importantly, we found that the act of codifying responsibilities in explicit detail hindered a proactive attitude and sense of communal ownership" (see Carr 2016). The danger is that employees don't get moving in the spirit of "just do it"; instead, they wait until their initiative has received a holacratic blessing. In the end, you run the risk of employees only doing "work according to holacratic rules."

4.4 Attempts to Formalize Interaction

The strong formal regulation of interactions in holacratic organizations is striking. Holacrats strictly distinguish between "tactical meetings," in which discussion focuses exclusively on decisions about next steps within an existing circle or a defined role, and "governance meetings," in which circles are adjusted and roles are redefined. To borrow from the sports jargon that is popular among both organizational scholars and organizational practitioners, "tactical meetings" are only about how to make "plays" within the existing set of rules, while "governance meetings" are about determining new rules within which plays can then be made (see Mitterer 2015, 426ff.).

Both the process of the "tactical meetings" and the "governance meetings" are predetermined down to the smallest detail. In "tactical meetings," after a check-in round according to a precisely specified order, the role bearers communicate the completion of tasks of individual roles, check the achievement of goals, give an update on current projects, and discuss tensions that are hindering the circle's work before the meeting ends with a check-out round (HolacracyOne 2013, 30–31). "Governance meetings" consist of a check-in round in which all participants share how they are currently feeling and provide their opening comments, followed by a clarification of administrative and logistical matters, the creation of an agenda for the meeting in which "tensions" can be dealt with, the working through of the agenda according to a predefined "integrative decision-making process," and end with a check-out round in which participants provide a concluding comment (HolacracyOne 2013, 19–20; German HolacracyOne 2015, 26–27).

The possibilities for deviation in both the "tactical meetings" and the "governance meetings" are low. As in agile software development, a mandatory "facilitator" ensures that the rules of interaction are strictly adhered to (see Eckstein and Muster 2021, 5). The holacratic governance software specifies for each individual meeting the order in which the individual points are to be worked through. It is not possible to deviate from this sequence.

Hoping Strict Rules Will Bring About Objectivity

In highly simplified terms, we can distinguish three forms that structure interaction in organizations. The first form of interaction is strongly influenced by superiors. They invite participants to the interaction, define the rules according to which the interaction will take place, and usually have the lion's share of speech in the interaction. This means that the participants in the interaction hold back a great deal or merely reformulate the superior's position in other words. The second variant is a low-structured interaction in which there are neither clear formal roles nor official rules. These interactions are dominated by the verbally extroverted, the rhetorically skilled, and the long-winded. This often results in unpredictable conflicts, meetings that get out of hand, and formulaic compromises found at the last moment. The third variant is a highly standardized interaction. Rules are set for the interaction, all participants are bound to the rules, and compliance is consistently enforced. These interactions are dominated by those who have mastered the formalized interaction rules in a particularly elegant manner.

At first glance, it seems surprising that highly standardized interaction formats are experiencing a renaissance, especially in organizational forms that are pretending to be modern. One would expect more low-structured forms of interactions in organizations that are striving to break themselves down into departments and dismantle hierarchies. We might expect more interaction formats in which the participants in the conversation set their own interaction rules. It would be more likely to assume that these organizations hope that groups will achieve ever greater maturity in shaping their interaction models through processes of self-organization (on such ideas in group dynamics, see Cronin 2015; Levi 2017).

At second glance, however, it becomes clear why organizations that want to do without steep hierarchies and clear departments seek their salvation in a strong standardization of the organization. Interactions without pronounced hierarchies and without limitations by departments can come apart very quickly factually, socially and temporally. There is erratic switching back and forth between factual topics, participants come and go, and meetings threaten to get out of hand in terms of time. The results that emerge from these discussions are often the result of random interactions.

The solution is therefore to strictly regulate the interaction. Instead of people reacting spontaneously to a problem description or solution proposal, a system is imposed in which they can only react in a precisely described way. Staff who have a problem or an idea for a solution should be given a "safe space" in which to work on it (see Robertson 2017).

Preparing the Interaction in Advance

This hyperformalized "corset" for interactions severely limits opportunities for open and free exchange, and restricts the space for creative development of ideas. One effect is that decisions are "discussed in advance and at least roughly agreed upon." The meetings of the circles are no longer used for discussion; they only deal with formalities. They become a formalized ritual. Everything important is negotiated before the circle meetings in casual, informal interactions that do not require legitimation of the speakers by sophisticated and complex rules.

Not infrequently, this results in an erosion of holacratic meetings. The interest in "tactical meetings" and "governance meetings" fades more and more and the official meetings take place less and less. Even a glance at the files stored in the holacratic governance software shows that, in many holacratic organizations, no "tactical meetings" or "governance meetings" have taken place for months. The unofficial preliminary votes for the official meetings seem to work so well that there is no longer any sense in holding them.

But in most cases, the holacratic meetings are adhered to. However, because so much has already been agreed upon in advance, meetings are "performed" in the "theater of organization," because "only the performance" provides the necessary holacratic legitimacy. Everyone knows their role in "the play." The proposal is introduced according to the holacratic rules, explained, "there is a discussion," and "pros and cons are exchanged, although all participants have long known all the arguments" (Matthiesen et al. 2022, 192).

4.5. The Rigidity of Holacratic Organizing Principles

The holacratic organizational principle is touted as the prototype of an evolutionary organization. Holacratic organizations were constantly adapting and self-correcting. "Anyone who senses the need for something in the organization to change" would know that there was a place to "take an idea and have it expressed" (Laloux 2014, 120).

The holacratic organizational model claims that the formal structure can be constantly adapted through a formalization process "from below." Simply changing the contours of roles and circles, as well as their tasks, should make it possible to adapt quickly to changing conditions. The result is supposed to be an incremental improvement of the formal structure, even in the face of continually changing framework conditions (see Robertson 2015a, 19ff.).

The Pitfalls of a Cross-Organizational Constitution

Although holacracy grants a great deal of flexibility in adapting circles, roles and tasks in the circles, individual organizations can only modify the basic principles of holacracy an extremely intense effort. The reason for this striking rigidity of holacratic organizations is that organizations cannot adapt the holacratic constitution on their own. In holacracy, the constitution serves as the guarantor that the organization does not creep back into an organizational structure bound by hierarchies and departments. By signing this constitution, an organization buys into the principle completely and thus secures holacracy in the organization.

The only way to adjust the constitution is for holacrats to agree world-wide on a new constitution. The first versions of the constitution were developed by one inventor of the concept alone; a whole series of advisors were involved in subsequent versions; and the last version was edited with the aid of software controls on the Internet. The revision process results in a new version of the constitution that holacratic organizations must adopt in its entirety.

Of course, one could object that no organization can be prevented from changing the constitution again with the stroke of a pen. However, this is actually blocked by the tight coupling between the holacratic constitution and the holacratic control software. The holacratic control software can only be modified when the consulting firm changes the constitution. Therefore, it is factually impossible for holacratic organizations to make even minor adjustments to the basic principles because this is not supported by the software.

On the Relationship Between Hyperstability and Hyperflexibility

Every organization faces the contradiction that it needs both redundancy and variance, but cannot strive for both at the same time (see Thompson 1967, 10ff.). Redundancy refers to the certainty with which you can assume that the bases for decisions remain stable, while variance points to the speed with which these bases can change (see Luhmann 1988, 173ff.). In this field of tension between redundancy and variance, every organization tries to find a middle way between the "self-paralysis of perfect order" and the "arbitrariness of perfect disorder" when designing its formal structure (Willke 1989, 96f.).

The striking thing about holacratic organizations is that they combine hyperstability, enshrined in the system's basic formal principles, with hyperflexibility in the detailed design of the formal structures within the overall framework. While the constitution defined in the cross-organizational governance software allows the organization to flexibly adjust circles and roles, modification of its basic formal structure comes about only at extremely high cost.

5.
Shadow Structures—Informal Correction Mechanisms in Holacratic Organizations

> "The irony of holacracy is that although it advocates freedom from an organizational system that can get in the way of work, the bureaucracy it replaces it with tends to be much more complicated to maintain. Undoubtedly one intention of a holacracy is to offer a lot of autonomy to the employees. Autonomy is a requirement for agility, a fact understood by the Mongols of Genghis Khan more than 800 years ago. But the Mongols achieved their unchallenged agility by keeping their processes to a minimum rather than expanding their regulations."
> *Vlademir Oane (2016) in an analysis of the abolition of holacracy at the companies Github, Medium and Buffer.*

Holacrats consider unproductive power struggles, everyday cronyism, and the primary transmission of information via water-cooler talk to be typical problems of classical organizations. Holacrats find that, in addition to formal structures, there are a variety of informal structures that always appear in classic organizations, and these often cannot be addressed.[47]

The promise of the holacratic model is that constant optimization can bring the formal and informal structures into alignment.[48] Instead of a formal organization chart that only exists on paper and an informal

---
47 Here, in their introductory seminars, holacrats choose the classic sales pitch for propagating new management concepts by asking interested people about the typical problems in their organizations, and then presenting the holacratic organizational model as a solution.
48 This is a description of the claim made by Zappos, one of the pioneering organizations in holacracy, which adopted the method in the early 2010s. See also Hsieh 2010.

organization chart that would map out the real organization, holacracy purports to deliver just one formal organization chart that is binding for all (see Groth 2013).[49]

The basic idea is that all of an organization's central expectations should be formalized for all to see so that no shadow structures can emerge. Similar to the way in which programming code specifies all requirements in a computer's operating system, all central processes and competencies must also be stored in the control software of holacracy, which serves as an operating system in organizations.

How plausible is this vision of extensive congruence between formal and informal structures in an organization?

5.1 The Formation of Shadow Structures in Holacratic Organizations

For classical organizations, which are based on the demarcation between departments and the formation of hierarchies, organizational research has found that the formal formation of expectations is always supplemented by an informal formation of expectations. Observers found that many expectations in organizations could not be formalized at all, which would inevitably lead to the formation of complementary and competing informal expectations. Furthermore, many formal expectations in organizations are not suitable for many situations, which leads to the construction of deviating informal expectations (Luhmann 1964, 27f.).

How does this interrelationship of formality and informality play out in organizations that are committed to dissolving departments and softening hierarchies in a holacratic constitution?

---

49 This hope for alignment between the formal and informal organizational charts may explain why holacrats have little use for a concept that has long been considered a central lever for controlling organizations: organizational culture. The approach to shaping organizational culture was a reactivation of an old governance fantasy: the dream of management through "collective programming of the mind" (Hofstede 1980, 13).

The Emergence of Shadow Departments

In holacratic organizations, more complex processes of division of labor are replaced by the principle of circles. Each circle is a self-organizing entity with its own rights. They are formed when a task cannot be performed by one role alone and systematic coordination between several roles is necessary. The principle of departments is formally undermined by the fact that an organizational member with completely different roles can be active in different circles (see Mitterer 2015). As a result, employees are assigned not to one department but to different circles, which—at least in the mind of the holacrats—undermines the typical silo formations that otherwise emerge.

What is more interesting from an organizational sociology perspective, however, is that the holacratic circle structure in many organizations ultimately reflects a classic departmental structure. In most holacratic organizations, members seem to be hired with a "primary role"—for example, as a programmer, as a financial manager, or as a human resources manager. As a result, in most cases, the majority of their working hours are done within one circle. This circle may also include staff, people with "lead" roles in other circles, but they will inevitably take on more ancillary or advisory roles.

In the holacratic control software, these factually existing departments are often not recognizable at first glance, but you can see them when you take a second look at the organization. When the organization moves into a new office space, the members who work together more frequently will form a table group, even if their regular cooperation is not represented by a circle. The table groups then give themselves their own names and decorate their table group with symbols that show that the employees here belong to a department that does not officially exist as a department at all.

The formation of departments in the operational core—i.e., the value-creating center of the organization—is particularly evident. Especially in project-based companies, which are managed via the holacratic organizational concept, the operational departments are often conspicuously "holacratically poor." The project teams are not, or only rudimentarily, mapped in the holacratic organizational structure, but are instead primarily coordinated via their own project management software. Project control then often takes place via a project manager who is responsible to the customer and distributes tasks to individual teams or team members (see also Hodgson 2004).[50]

In holacratic organizations, silo formation can be further reinforced by control via "dashboards," which are management cockpits that show central key figures. Performance data—for example, hours billed to the customer—is systematically collected for the project teams. This leads teams to focus primarily on achieving the specified performance targets and to isolate themselves from the rest of the organization.

This can lead to a paradox: setting up agile project structures in an organization undermines its basic holacratic principles. In line with agile project management logic, fixed teams are formed that control themselves with the support of scrum masters and product owners, coordinate daily in stand-up meetings with the same employees, and reflect on difficulties with other team members in retrospectives. These agile work forms work against the holacratic structure with their formation of fixed teams that develop their own silos.

Informal silo formation in holacratic organizations can be loosened up by bringing members together in specialist-oriented communities that exist outside the activities with which they spend the majority of their time. Circles are then formed for this purpose, in which, for example, the professional exchange of specialists from different teams or the development of further training formats can take place. In fact, we find a very similar situation when, in classic organizations, specialists who are operationally active in interdisciplinary teams are enabled to exchange professional ideas with other specialists in the field in a parallel structure.[51]

---

50 Here it would be interesting to see, especially with regard to the holacratic pioneer company Zappos, whether the areas central to the company, such as IT, were managed according to holacratic principles.
51 See the management literature on the formal formation of communities of practices, for example Wenger and Snyder 2000. As an introduction, see Wenger 1999.

The Differentiation of Shadow Hierarchies

Despite all the anti-hierarchy rhetoric, the holacratic constitution has a basic hierarchical structure.[52] The anchor circle—the General Company Circle—determines the lead link positions in all subordinate circles and in effect acts as the top of the organization. Because the company founders, capital owners and former managers play an important role in the anchor circle, there is an opportunity to influence work in the subordinate circles by means of filling the lead link positions.

The central point here, however, is that from the basic holacratic perspective, it is a role-related, not a person-related, hierarchy. This means that the lead link's options for exerting influence relate only to the person in his or her function as a role bearer in a circle, not to the person as a whole. Particularly when organizational members take on different roles in different circles, there are hardly any similarities in this role-based hierarchy with the formal structure of the person-based hierarchies of classic organizations.

It is interesting to note, however, that a person-based hierarchy often emerges in the shadow of the holacratic formal structure (see Goyk and Grote 2018; Martela 2019; Schell and Bischof 2022; Brodda 2023; Sua-Ngam-Iam 2023b).[53] In the simplest version, it takes place—in a holacratically correct manner—through the combination of central roles in individual people. At the moment when one person holds the roles of the signatory for central orders, the internal work distributor, the decision maker on salary increases, and that of the person who fires people, this role bearer has in fact assumed a leadership role.[54]

In smaller holacratic organizations, shadow hierarchies often operate directly. The central roles are taken by the founders, who coordi-

---

52   See Lee and Edmondson 2017, 39, but without systematically distinguishing between formal and informal aspects of hierarchy. On the anti-hierarchy rhetoric of the holacrats, see already the subtitle of the English paperback version of the book by Brian Robertson (2015b): "The Revolutionary Management System that Abolishes Hierarchy."
53   On the formation of informal hierarchies and further research perspectives, see Diefenbach and Sillince 2011, 1532.
54   On the reverse process—contrasting a formal hierarchy with an informal hierarchy—see for example Aghion and Tirole 1997.

nate informally. If the founders hold the majority of the capital in the company, all employees know that they can take back the holacratic principles with a stroke of the pen, and they anticipate this in their decisions. Employees make the decisions they imagine the founders would make, or they discuss them with the founders so that in the end these decisions only have to undergo a holacratic approval process.[55]

However, the formation of hierarchical shadow structures is also evident in larger holacratic companies. For example, the analyses show that holacracy does not abolish all of the bosses in the company; it merely does away with all bosses except for the CEO. The "radical new management policy," according to the analysis, would have transformed the company into "a dictatorship" instead of "a democracy" (thus Carr 2015b). The effect of holacracy's consistent decentralization is a de facto centralization of decision-making power.

The informal centralization of power in holacratic organizations has a serious consequence. The top of the organization is in danger of being overloaded with decision-making demands. Therefore, in larger holacratic organizations, an informal hierarchical parallel structure based on staff develops in the shadow of a formal basic structure with little hierarchy.

In this shadow hierarchy, less experienced employees are each assigned to an experienced employee. These experienced employees—called "Personnel Excellence Leads" or "Human Success Advisors" depending on the organization—are then responsible for challenging and sponsoring the employees assigned to them. However, the Personnel Excellence Leads or Human Success Advisors not only advise employees on their development in the organization, but also contribute to decisions on salary reductions or increases and have a significant influence on whether or not a person assigned to them is terminated.

The employees who act as informal managers in the organization are usually responsible for eight to twelve organizational members and, due to their management tasks, have to invoice smaller shares of their

---

[55] A recurrently thematized effect arises from corporate law that management is liable regardless of the internal structuring of the organization. However, responsibility can also arise from management's accountability to external owners of capital, for example when a startup has been purchased by a larger company or loans are taken out with banks.

working time to the customer. At first glance, this shadow hierarchy is concealed by the representation generated by the holacratic software. At second glance, the similarity to the classic model of hierarchy with disciplinary superiors, which forms alongside a structure of specialist superiors, cannot be overlooked.[56]

5.2 The Thing with Transparency

In many classical organizations, claims to transparency only have meaning on the display side; however, in holacratic organizations, these claims to transparency are implemented at the operational level. Holacratic software makes all deliberations, discussion processes, and decisions in the organization visible to all employees at all times. This transparency refers not only to the circles in which one is active oneself, but also to all other circles. Transparency is implemented almost ideally in holacratic organizations due to the control exercised through the operating software (see Minnaar and van Vondelen 2022, 137).

In many cases, the demand for transparency is not limited to the processes prescribed by the holacratic constitution; it frequently extends to other central processes as well. The organization's software enables employees to access not only the financial situation and status of all projects, but also the qualifications and compensation of all employees (see Laloux 2014, 217).

Going further, it is not uncommon for all organizational members to be viewable, in detail, online via the Circles, Roles and Tasks. All you have to do is go via the Internet to a person who is presented there, and then you can view the roles, members, policies, notes, projects, key figures, checklists and discussion histories of all circles, in detail, using the "All my roles" function. How do transparency claims play out in the practice of holacratic organizations?

---

56 In one organization we studied, an employee put it succinctly, "Human Success Advisors at our company are people who are called managers at other companies" (Kühl 2023).

The Formation of Backstage Areas

Despite all of their noble claims, holacratic organizations clarify central questions on non-transparent backstage areas that lurk behind a front stage oriented toward transparency. Important decisions are not discussed in the holacratic structure; they are pre-decided in closed channels in the organization's internal communication system. The founders, who at least formally disempower themselves by introducing the holacratic constitution, meet in messenger services outside the organization, where decisions for the holacratic organization are prepared. Blacklists of employees that the organization intends to terminate are kept outside of the official filing systems.

We know from organizational research that organizations characterized by strong demands for transparency form distinctive cultures of informal coordination (for more on this, see in detail Kühl 2022, 159ff.)). Instead of filing documents on official drives, people keep separate lists and schedules on their computers that are not readily accessible. Instead of communicating briefly in writing, people agree on relevant points only in face-to-face communications, because this makes it less likely that traces will be left in the files. "Sofa cultures" emerge in which votes no longer take place in formal meetings for which minutes are taken, but only in informal, undocumented circles (see the case studies on this, for example, in Roberts 2006; Ringel 2018).

The Transparency Paradox of Holacratic Organizations

In organizational research, this effect is referred to as the *transparency paradox*. The more transparency is demanded in the organization, the stronger the efforts are to hide. In the formal structure, everything is made accessible in organizations covered by transparency measures. Processes are generally visible, documents are accessible, and instructions are written down in memos. Distinct "checkmark cultures" are formed in which organizational members must constantly confirm that they have taken note of a piece of information, followed a procedure, or performed an action (see O'Neill 2010).[57] However, this is accompanied on the informal side by increasingly opaque information and documentation processes. File wastelands are deliberately produced in which sensitive information is untraceable, or superficial Power Point presentations are filed as minutes to prevent accurate documentation. Sensitive comments are attached with Post-It notes because they can be removed before archiving (on these strategies, see Hood 2007, 204). The result of efforts to achieve internal transparency is then not the hoped-for disappearance of the organization's backstage of the organization but, on the contrary, the formation of a particularly cleverly hidden backstage.

These informal communication channels can develop such a dynamic that, in the shadow of extensive transparency, entire parts of the company prepare their exit from the organization. Thus it could happen that, in a consulting firm that has adopted the holacratic transparency criteria, consultants plan their own holacratic consulting organization without the knowledge of the rest of the organization, surprise everyone else overnight with their departure, and the remaining ones wonder how such a spin-off is possible in a holacratic system that is supposed to make tensions transparent for everyone.

Holacratic organizations are a prime example of organizations becoming simultaneously much more and much less transparent (for more on this phenomenon, see Osrecki 2015, 355).[58] Every member of the organization gets deep insights into the formal expectations of the organization via the IT systems and at the same time has to spend a lot of time understanding and using the well-hidden informal expectations.

---

57 On this kind of box-ticking culture in organizations, see also McGivern and Ferlie 2007 or Larner and Mason 2014.
58 See also the empirically impressive study by Bernstein 2012. For a similar argument from the perspective of principal-agent theory, see Prat 2005.

5.3 Advantages and Disadvantages of Holacratic Shadow Structures

It is not surprising, from an organizational science perspective, that a variety of informal structures emerge to compensate for the hyperformalization that predominates in holacratic organizations. Certainly, the holacratic organizational model claims to address the dysfunctionalities of the formal structure through the identification of tensions and to transfer them into an improved structure through decisions. However, this does not change the fact that opposing informal processes repeatedly form precisely at critical points.

Functionalities of a Shadow Structure

We are familiar with how highly formalized organizations, which rely on delimited departments and pronounced hierarchies, create informal structures to compensate for the dysfunctionalities caused by formal structures. The pronounced silo formation through formally separated departments is balanced in informality by stable "short official channels" through which the cooperation of the departments is coordinated outside of the formal structure. The hierarchical structure of top-down instructions and supervision of superiors is mitigated by informally preparing the decisions that are made at the top, and then ensuring that the right decisions are made at the top by unobtrusively "supervising" superiors.

The central difference of these informal countermovements in holacratic organizations—and this is the central insight for organizational science—is that, due to the proclaimed formal abolition of hierarchies and departments, these countervailing structures then emerge on an informal basis. While in organizations based on the unambiguous assignment of people to departments, a variety of informal arrangements are established across departmental boundaries, in holacratic organizations, informal closure mechanisms materialize in the face of the formally established openness of circles. While in organizations based on the clear assignment of staff in hierarchically arranged communication channels, the informal compensation consists in the formation of informal supervision processes of superiors running counter to the formal hierarchy, in holacratic organizations, informal hierarchies are formed running counter to the formal equalization processes.

The shadow structures of holacratic organizations fulfill an important function. They reintroduce principles, in an informal way, with the differentiation of completed departments and the formation of personal hierarchies that are discredited in holacratic management discourse, but nevertheless serve important functions for the organization. The differentiation of departments with clear assignment of staff ensures that organizational members can focus on a sub-goal without their attention being diverted by other organizational sub-goals. The formation of personal hierarchy enables decisions to be made and implemented quickly, even decisions that are unpleasant for the organization.

The Dysfunctionality of the Shadow Structure

But this formation of informal structures inevitably brings with it dysfunctionalities for the organization. Compared to classical organizations, the taboo organizational processes have changed fundamentally. In classical organizations, it is possible to refer to the principles of department and hierarchy in internal coordination. For all the anti-department and anti-hierarchy rhetoric on the surface, it is widely accepted in most organizations that departments focus on their work and that hierarchical superiors make unpleasant decisions. In holacratic organizations, however, the principles of departmentalization and hierarchy are so formally blocked by the signing of the constitution that it is not possible in internal processes to refer to these mechanisms, which now exist only in informality.

The main problem of informal action deviating from formal expectations is that this phenomenon largely escapes rationalization (Luhmann 1964, 314). Deviations from the holacratic formal structure often cannot even be openly addressed. Particularly in organizations with strong shadow hierarchies, it is possible to complain on the backstage about the influence of the founders and owners of capital, which goes far beyond the formal structure, but this can only be addressed in larger rounds at a high personal risk.[59]

When the shadow structures are openly addressed, however, they almost inevitably acquire a critical undertone due to the organization's commitment to the holacratic constitution. If informal departments or informal hierarchies develop in holacratic organizations, then according to holacratic logic they must be abolished. It would not do to informally institute the principles that you want to abolish with holacracy. So if shadow structures exist that run counter to the holacratic ones, they would have to be abolished or at least weakened. The consequence is that this pushes the often functional informal mechanisms even further into the taboo area.

This creates the effect that in holacratic organizations, which as a basic formal principle places the importance of role over person, great importance is given to the informal formation of expectations of a person (see Sua-Ngam-Iam 2023b). This brings the advantage for a holacratic organization that expectation security can be established not only through role definitions but also through knowledge of the person, but it makes the organization vulnerable to changes of staff. Basically, as Niklas Luhmann already pointed out, "every deviation from formal rules" cancels the "separation of office and person"—or holacratically speaking, of role and person (Luhmann 1964, 313). This makes action personal in a way, but this is precisely what hyperformalists want to prevent.

---

59 The founders wonder why certain conversations in the coffee corner fall silent, even though they believe they have relinquished a significant amount of their power by signing the holacratic constitution.

5.4 The Change Between Formality and Informality as a Competence

While holacratic practitioners concede to the formation of shadow structures, they are seen as a weakness in the implementation of a holacratic organization. Since the basic idea of holacracy is precisely to prevent the formation of departmental silos and to dissolve staff hierarchy, these informal compensations within the holacratic structure are seen as a problem and not a solution. Holacratic practitioners believe that the informal structures that contradict holacratic principles should be addressed through the articulation of tensions and then holacratically put in order.

Behind this is the old dream in management that organizations can be perfected through ever more clever formalizations to such an extent that they are optimally adapted to changing environmental conditions. At the same time, their proponents admit that the path to an optimal formal structure for the organization is repeatedly blocked by implementation obstacles, acclimatization difficulties and resistance movements. But all of this, they say, should not distract from the fact that organizations are walking the walk. If only the change process is designed well enough, if only employees receive sufficient training and if the right consultants are engaged, then the difficulties of the transformation can be overcome.

From an organizational science perspective, one can have doubts about this drive for ever further perfection. Organizations cannot exist as a "completely formalized system." This is not because of a "lack of perfection," but because an organization in which all expectations were formally represented would not be "viable at all." (Luhmann 1964, 27). The formation of informal structures, which often run counter to the formal structures, are necessary balancing movements in the organization in order to maintain viability in the face of all efforts at formalization.

Organizational performance is not primarily the result of everyone fine-tuning their formal structure to ever greater perfection, but rather of a high degree of sensitivity to the tension between formal and informal expectations in organizations. Instead of changing formal structures in ever more elaborate, ever more participatory processes, the organizational skill of many members seems to lie in switching back and forth between formal and informal expectations in a way that moves the organization forward.

6.
On the Rise and Fall of a Management Fashion

"Management by Book Report"
Comment of a management consultant on the offer of then-CEO of Zappos, Tony Hsieh, to pay three full months' salary to all employees who want to leave the company after the introduction of holacracy—provided they have read the book "Reinventing Organizations" by Frederic Laloux first.
(see Carr 2015a; see also Groth 2018b, 146f.)

It is hard to ignore the management fads that have been promoted as panaceas in recent decades.[60] As criticism grew of the bureaucratic model of organization after World War II, the "organic enterprise form" (Burns and Stalker 1961), the "synthetic organization" (J. D. Thompson 1967) and "adhocracy" (Toffler 1971) became fashionable.[61] This was followed by the promotion of "Theory Z" (Ouchi 1981), "Model J" (Aoki 1990) and "System 5" (Likert and Araki 1986) or the "integrative-innovative system" (Kanter 1983).

After these notions faded away, the reduction of hierarchical levels and the dissolution of departmental silos were then subsumed under new formulas such as the "multicellular organization" (Landier 1987), the "lean enterprise" (Womack, Jones, and Ross 1990) and the

---

60 This is a preliminary ordering of a selection of management concepts from both a more consulting and a more scientific context. One seems to be able to produce effects in publications simply by listing the multitude of new and old organizational concepts. See for an early variant DiMaggio 2001.
61 The proposed term "Adhocracy" in "Future Shock" by Alvin Toffler 1971 is interesting in that it was taken up in organizational science by Henry Mintzberg. See also Mintzberg 1988 or Mintzberg and McHugh 1985. See also for the prominent treatment of adhocracy in his structural concept Mintzberg 1980 and comprehensively Mintzberg 1983.

"reengineered enterprise" (Hammer and Champy 1993). Consultants peddled new ideas such as the "modular factory" (Wildemann 1988), the "fractal factory" (Warnecke 1992), the "responsive organization" (Coulson-Thomas and Brown 1989) and the "required organization" (Jaques 1989).

While these concepts expressed hopes for a well-done form of thorough formalization, other ideas, such as the "learning organization" (Senge 1990), the "intelligent organization" (Landier 1991), the "knowledge-generating enterprise" (Nonaka and Takeuci 1995) or the "collaborative enterprise" (Campbell and Goold 2000) emphasized the importance of informality in organizations. Other terms such as the "multicellular enterprise" (Landier 1987), the "centerless corporation" (Pasternack and Viscio 1998), the "boundaryless organization" (Ashkenas et al. 1995), the "horizontal organization" (Ostroff 1999) and the "self-managed organization" (Purser and Cabana 1998) envisioned the dissolution of hierarchy and the permeability of departments.

As these management concepts ran out of steam, not least due to the crises in the capital markets, the idea of post-bureaucratic organizations was then reinvented under new names. The word-creation machinery of management consultants produced such shorthand phrases as "agile organization" (following Beck et al. 2001), "adaptive organization" (Fulmer 2000), "resilient organization" (Välikangas 2010), "teal organization" (Laloux 2014), "holacratic organization" (Robertson 2015b), "conversational company" (Turco 2016), "collegially led organization" (Oestereich and Schröder 2017) and "beta organization" (Hermann and Pfläging 2020).

How does holacracy fit into this endless stream of management concepts? In what ways does the propagation of holacracy as a management concept resemble the application of other management fashions? What function do management fads like holacracy serve in organizations? What will be the future of hyperformalized organizational concepts?

6.1 On the Making of Management Fashions

One approach to management fashions from an organizational science perspective is to describe in detail their mode of operation in organizations. The rather flowery language of the advocates of management fashions, and their ignoring of the history of similar concepts, means that their basic principles are not always immediately recognizable. They dispense with theoretical classification of the basic principles in order not to scare off practitioners and not to jeopardize the dramatization of one's own model as something previously unknown. Here, the task of organizational science is to describe the basic principles of this management fashion in such a way that they can be related to the extensive research on organizations.

In addition to this translation of management fashions into a language that can be connected to organizational science findings, another approach from organizational science is to deconstruct the way management fashions are made. In doing so, it is important to take a closer look at the ingredients that come together to make management fashions. It is striking that regardless of whether a management fad aims to increase flexibility, innovation and efficiency through more informality—"Model I"—or through more formality—"Model F"—they use the same rhetorical tricks.

Dramatization of Social Challenges

Dramatic societal changes often serve to justify a new management fashion. The world is ostensibly moving faster and faster, processes are becoming more and more complex, forecasts are becoming more and more uncertain, and decision-makers are being confronted with developments that are becoming more and more difficult to assess (see Kotter 2014, 3ff.). There is talk of an increasing scarcity of raw materials, a growing danger from terrorist attacks and regionally limited wars, an increase in natural disasters, impending ecological collapse, an increase in debt, a shortage of time as a resource, and growing social inequality.

This acknowledges that in the industrial age, the old model of "predict and control" still seems to have worked. In the past, according to one of the main promoters of holacracy, companies achieved both "enduring stability" and "growing successes" "through up-front planning, centralized control, and the prevention of deviation." The idea would have been based on developing "the 'perfect' system" in advance to avoid tensions (Robertson 2015a, 12f.). But in the post-industrial world, according to the usual argument of inventors of management fashions, we now face fundamentally "new challenges" such as "growing complexity, increasing transparency, greater interconnectedness at all levels, shorter time horizons, economic and ecological instability" (Robertson 2015a, 13).

In their contemporary diagnoses, the promoters of management fashions emphasize that there have never been such fundamental social changes as there are now. Whether one takes a management fashion from the early 1920s, the post-World War II period, the 1970s marked by the oil shock, the 1990s defined by the end of the Cold War, the pre-turn-of-the-century period dominated by strong inflows of venture capital, or the 2010s, they always insist that there has never been a time when technological upheaval, economic challenges, and social dislocation have been as fundamental as they are now. Even if they concede that there have been profound changes before, they always suggest that we are living in particularly turbulent times right now that demand an urgent response from organizations. There is an unmistakable tone of alarmism in management fads.

The Proclamation of Revolutionary Change

Classical organizational models, according to the dramatization that usually accompanies management concepts, "often fail to provide the agility desired and needed in this landscape of rapid change and dynamic complexity." The general tenor implies that "today's organizations," are "obsolete" (Robertson 2015a, 13). Those who cling to outdated organizational principles—according to the monotonously repeated theme of management fad promoters—risk the "penalty of doom."

Checklists of "warning signs" offer a method to assess whether organizations are "outdated." Is there "distrust and frustration between colleagues"? Are important tasks being "overlooked"? Are there "many meetings with lengthy discussions to reach consensus"? Are emails circulating with many people "included in the cc line, often for unclear reasons"? Do employees "consult before making a decision"? Do employees have "lots of ideas about" what should be done, but without doing it themselves? Because these effects usually occur automatically in organizations based on the division of labor, going through these checklists must make every manager worry that they may not have noticed the "winds of change" (example from Robertson 2015b, 39).

What management fashion sponsors then demand is nothing less than a revolutionary change in the way organizations structure themselves. Management gurus, organizational consultants, and even some organizational scholars do not hesitate to invoke the "need for a revolution" (Peters 1988, 3ff.), a "real revolution" (Crozier 1989, 21) or even a "cultural revolution (Landier 1991). Appeals to management appear under such titles as "directions for revolutionaries" (Tichy 1995), "manifestos for business revolutions" (Hammer and Champy 1993) and "manuals for a management revolution" (Peters 1988). Management fashions are presented as a "new management system for a rapidly changing world" (Robertson 2015a, 1).

Thinking in Terms of Maturity

Most management fashions work with a more or less simplistically constructed progress model to chart the path towards a revolutionary management system. Organizations then evolve in this framework, for example, away from the model of a "pack" dominated by a boss that makes all the decisions, the model of an "army" characterized by obedient regularity, or the model of an "organization" oriented primarily toward efficiency, and towards the conception of a "family" that combines classical hierarchy and a high degree of autonomy, until they finally become the epitome of a "network" consisting of self-organizing units (see Laloux 2014).[62]

Such models of organizational forms permanently evolving for the better can easily be combined with the development of leadership roles. The notion of the big boss with a strict hierarchy is followed, the narrative goes, by the idea of two-way leadership, in which classic top-down leadership is combined with shared leadership. After the formation of shared management comes the principle of democratic leadership, according to which employees elect their bosses themselves, ultimately ending in leaderless organizations characterized by absolute equality among all members (see Bruch and Berger 2016).

Sometimes the development stages are highlighted with colors to make it even easier to locate them. A magenta organization with an impulsive leadership style would be followed by an amber-yellow system dominated by formal leadership, which would be replaced by an orange structure characterized by performance. This would then be followed by a green organization characterized by participation, which in the final stage would lead to a blue-green shimmering enterprise characterized by completely new forms of cooperation (see the colorful presentation in Laloux 2014).

---

62 The roots of this thinking in the "spiral dynamics" of the "integral approach" cannot be discussed in detail here. The integral approach is ultimately a concept in which everything that exists in scientific, philosophical, and religious approaches is brought together: systems theory, neurobiology, Jungian archetypes, hermeneutics, Hegelian dialectics, Zen Buddhism, neoliberalism, poststructuralism, neo-Hinduism, transpersonal states of consciousness, and Neoplatonism (see Manson 2020). The result should be, according to the supporters of the integral approach, a comprehensive concept that extracts anything that is useful and seems meaningful from existing structures of thought (see Wilber 2000; for a critique see Meyerhoff 2010; for dealing with this criticism, see Wilber 2006). Because of this claim, convinced holacrats then also describe their first encounter with the integral approach as a "cognitive orgasm." "All of the knowledge" accumulated up to this point crystallizes in the "head abruptly in the form of a coherent figure" (Wittrock 2020, v). A personal meeting with Ken Wilber, one of the founders of the integral approach, is then compared to an encounter with Einstein or Hegel, "only cooler" (Wittrock 2020, vi). The revelatory dimension of this revival experience becomes fully understandable only when you think that meeting Einstein or Hegel—at least if we are to believe the biographers—must have been pretty "cool" as well. On meeting Einstein, see the biography of Fölsing 2013; for Hegel, see Kaube 2020.

These more or less explicit suggestions of progress have an important function for management fashions, every one of which threatens to signal a failure of management. After all, management has not yet introduced the principle promoted by the management fashion and has thus exposed their organization to risk. However, by presenting the principle as the next stage in a model of progress, managers are reassured that, by adapting the management fashion, they are merely taking the next step in the organization's evolution towards something (even) better.

The Salvation of the Individual, the Organization and the Whole World

Social processes are usually characterized by the fact that what benefits one group harms another. When salaries are cut, this is at the expense of workers, but for employers it has benefits because of the cost savings. When automobile companies try to influence politicians to set the limits for emissions as high as possible, this has advantages for them because they save costs for exhaust gas treatment, but for city dwellers it brings disadvantages in the form of increased incidence of asthma, strokes or heart attacks. Many advantages can only be achieved because the disadvantages are externalized , which means they are passed on to others. In game theory, this is called a zero-sum game. The gain of one can only be achieved by the loss of another.

In contrast to the view that the benefit of some is the harm of others, management fashions promise that with their support these zero-sum games can be interrupted. By implementing their central principle in organizations, they promise, everyone would ultimately benefit. Employees will become happier, organizations more efficient, customers more satisfied because of better quality products. The community will benefit from more innovative organizations, the environment will be less polluted, and the world as a whole will become a better place. In game theory, this is called a win-win situation. The gain of some also represents a gain for others.

In management fads, this notion of a win-win situation is particularly evident in the promises of happiness that refer to both the meso level of the organization and the micro level of each individual. The concept no longer promises just an improvement in effectiveness, efficiency, and innovation in an organization; it also assures the enablement of growth potential for individuals. Holacracy, convinced holacrats argue, is a "Trojan horse." People are looking for ideas to "make organizations more effective and efficient." You'd get that, too—"in droves." But it would also "open the door" to "a new terrain of reality" within oneself, to a "new evolutionary potential" that "lies dormant in every human being, just waiting to be activated" (Wittrock 2020, vii). Holacratic meetings promise to provide "powerful opportunities for personal growth." The "whole meeting structure at holacracy" is designed to bring to light the "unprocessed issues," the "projections," the "egos." These aspects become "simply visible, clear and transparent" and can thus "dissolve naturally" (Brian Robertson in an interview in Laloux 2014, 164).

But society as a whole, according to the ever-repeated promise, would also benefit fundamentally. Holacrats argue that companies with a traditional organizational form have an "unhealthy autonomy" and ignore their "responsibility to the broader world" (Robertson 2006, 15).[63] Holacracy would have the potential, "without any messy revolutions," to transcend our classical notion of national governments into a new type of "world-wide integrative power structure" (Robertson 2006, 4). It would create a "new kind of integrated nervous system and decision-making nexus for the world" (Robertson 2006, 19). The end result would be a better world with more prosperity, less pollution, and fewer conflicts.[64]

---

63 The original states, "Our current corporate governance model pushes the company-level holon toward unhealthy autonomy—it is encouraged to ignore its responsibilities to the broader world" (Robertson 2006, 15).

64 The initial connection of holacracy to the integral approach is also evident in this argument. "Holacracy" is a combination of the "*Hola*-rchy" *of* Arthur Koestler and Ken Wilber and the "Socio-*cracy*" of sociocrat Gerard Endenburg. Ken Wilber, one of the masterminds of the integral approach, had, in the style of Arthur Koestler (1967, 58), described "holarchy" as an order in which each higher level is more integral than the previous level, because

The Presentations of a Recipe for Success

The options that organizations have to give themselves a shape are straightforward. They can tend towards decentralizing decisions to find locally adapted solutions, or to centralize them to streamline the organization. Organizations can flatten hierarchies while accepting wider spans of leadership, or work more with steep hierarchies to ensure executive responsiveness. You can try to secure long-term staff commitment to the organization to benefit from their loyalty, or instead focus on high staff interchangeability to maintain higher staff flexibility. Employees can be managed with precise if-then rules and thus achieve a high degree of work routinization, or by setting targets and leaving the means of fulfilling goals to the employees themselves.

In total, there are a few dozen adjusting screws in organizations that can be turned in one direction or another.[65] Management fads tend to single only one of these well-known principles out and then pretend that it is the key factor in an organization's success (see Kieser 1996, 23): the decomposition of the work process into the smallest possible packages (Taylor 1967); internal entrepreneurship (Pinchot 1988); the reduction of buffers (Womack et al. 1990); the organizational culture (Peters and Waterman 1982); the optimization of processes (Hammer and Champy 1993); or, as in the case of holacracy, the importance of the role (Robertson 2015a).

However, sometimes it may make sense for organizations to start with one of these adjusting screws to address specific problems in

---

a holon is both "a whole" and "a part" (Wilber 1995, 26). Only the ending "-archy", which refers to the character of rule, was replaced by the ending "-cracy," which refers more strongly to the form of control (Robertson 2015a, 37). Early presentations pointed out that the genesis of the term holacracy originated "with the help of Ken Wilber" (Robertson 2006, 5). This adoption of Ken Wilber's concept is no longer mentioned in the "History of Holacracy" by Brian Robertson (2014, 8).

65 Contingency theory—also called the situational approach—was a separate research direction that tried to collect and describe as many of these adjusting screws as possible, but made the mistake of thinking that they could say for every environmental situation which adjusting screws have to be turned and how (see as a quick overview Alexy 2022). This research tradition has largely disappeared, but the hope to find the right adjusting screws still shimmers through in institutional economic approaches.

individual organizational units. What is striking, however, is how this specific solution becomes generalized into a guiding principle for the entire organization. The idea of doing away with a supervisor in teamwork and electing a spokesperson instead may make sense, but this is then hyped up as a principle for the entire organization under the idea of a democratic enterprise. The basic idea of agile programming methods—that software development proceeds on the basis of week-to-week goals instead of a planning process extending over months or years—has its plausibility in that context, but then the concept of the agile organization is universalized as a guiding principle for the entire organization. The idea of defining the roles of organizational members down to the smallest detail was successfully tested on assembly lines and call centers, and holacracy elevates this to a basic principle for the entire organization.

The Praise of Pioneering Organizations

Proclaiming a principle for success is not enough on its own. We also need assurance that such principles also work. Therefore, it is essential to the establishment of a management fashion that we have testimonials from organizations that have become successful through the principle. It must appear as if "real managers" have solved "real problems" in "real organizations" with this principle (Clark and Greatbatch 2016, 413). The presentation of pioneering organizations that can be used to illustrate the application of management principles plays a central role in management fads (Miller et al. 2004, 14).

The simplest way to identify a vanguard organization is for consultants to present their own company as a vanguard organization (on this phenomenon, see Kühl 2020a, 179). In this case, we have the consulting firm's own application of the method, as well as the successes they have cultivated with this method. Even in the case of Business Process Engineering, consulting firms touted the method by saying that it had tripled their own efficiency. With Lean Management, consulting firms also claimed that the streamlining of their own company had led to a strong reduction in costs. With holacracy, consulting firms took this principle of applying a method in one's own organization to the extreme as a marketing tool.[66]

All consulting firms offering the implementation of holacracy as a product pointed out that they also use the method themselves and have had positive experiences (see Robertson 2015a, 16).[67] When we take a took at the lists of holacratic pioneer organizations, the high portion of small consulting firms with a handful of coworkers is worth noting, particularly since it is often the case that they only offer one product: the introduction of holacratic organization models (first noticed by Zeuch 2016a). In the management books that tout holacracy as a model for the twenty-first century, micro-organizations of consultants appear to be the model for the organization of the future, despite the claim that such firms claim to focus only on large organizations, (see the especially striking passages in Laloux 2014, 122, 129, 182, 217, 257f., 267, 304).

But consultants pointing to their own positive experience with a method that they themselves sell is not sufficient evidence to propel a management fashion to the fore. Therefore, they identify pioneer organizations aside from their their own. There are two different variants in this strategy. The first version subjects organizations that are considered progressive to an analysis, and then presents the consultants' own recipes as the result (for this, see e.g. Peters and Waterman 1982 and Peters and Waterman 1983; Collins 2001; Laloux 2014). The second version presents a collection of recipes for success and then illustrates

---

66 The commercialization of a management fashion could be well examined in the case of holacracy. A consulting firm that holds the trademark rights controls modifications to the constitution. Consultants who want to introduce holacracy under this brand name have to undergo training, acquire licenses as holacracy consultants, and renew them regularly. Ultimately, holacracy is an attempt to turn a management concept into a kind of franchise model. As with McDonalds, Burger King, or Subway, franchisees acquire the right to introduce holacracy into organizations under that name in exchange for a seal of quality from the company controlling the brand. In return, the franchisees attend training courses at the brand-controlling companies for a fee and undergo regular follow-up training by these companies. In doing so, they sell software to the companies they advise, which in turn benefits the company from which the certificates as official holacracy consultants are acquired.
67 "We eat our own dog food" (Robertson 2015a, 16).

the approach's impact with the example of organizations that have been successful in using these methods (for this, see e.g. Womack et al.1990; Hammer and Champy 1993; Robertson 2015b).[68]

Often, we don't find out about the data underlying the representation of pioneering organizations. We don't know how many interviews were conducted in the organization, which participant observations were carried out, and how the organization's documents were evaluated. Instead, a more or less well-done "storytelling" dominates (see March 2016, 56f.). The pioneering organizations are presented in the most illustrative language possible, the depictions are characterized by the struggle with dramatic crises, and there is always an impressive happy ending at the end.

Storytelling's central function is to personalize an organization's success story (see on the following examples Kieser 1997, 58). We are talking about the discovery of Lean Management at the car manufacturer Toyota by the later CEO Eiji Toyoda and his "production genius" Taiichi Ohno (Womack et al. 1990, 53); Percy Barnevik's vision of a consistently decentralized form of organization, developed by the CEO of the automation and energy company ABB (Peters 1992, 45); or Tony Hsieh, who is said to have led his company Zappos to new vistas with holacracy (Robertson 2015a, 18f.; see also Hsieh 2010 for his own book).

The stories about vanguard organizations establish a simple causal relationship between an organization's supposed success and a management principle (see March 2016, 54ff.). Increases in efficiency, innovation, or employee satisfaction are attributed in a highly simplistic way to the application of a management principle. Such storytelling ignores the fact that completely different factors—a general economic upswing, a change in management or even just a lucky coincidence—could have contributed to the organization's success (see Huczynski 2006, 232).

The stories about pioneering organizations then spread via a simple copy and paste. In a best-selling management book, an organization

---

68 For holacracy, several organizations such as Ternary, Medium, Gifhorn, and Zappos serve to illustrate the method's success. The online retailer Zappos, in particular, played an important role in demonstrating that the method can be applied to organizations with more than a thousand employees (see Laloux 2014, 175; Laloux 2015, 177).

that the authors have, at best, become acquainted with through a brief visit and a few conversations, is praised as a case study of their management principle.[69] Then a process in which others adopt this case study, in a largely unexamined way, sets in. Consultants who jump on a fad present the organization discussed in a management bestseller as a model, often without having done any analysis of their own. Managers who try to use a management fad in their own organization present the organization covered in the management bestseller as a role model, even though at best they have only seen the display side of the organization during a company tour lasting a maximum of one day.

In the process of retelling a story, the image of the organization as a pioneer of a management principle is solidified. If a story is told so often, the assumption goes, then it can't be wrong. The effect is that literature about these pioneering organizations haunts the management discussion for years—sometimes decades—even though it often has little to do with the organization that was once originally praised in the management bestseller.[70]

6.2 The Outsourcing of Responsibility— on the Function of Management Fashions

The genesis of management fads bears strong similarities to religions (arguing along these lines, see Krell 1994, 276ff.; Furnham 2004, 4; Greatbatch and Clark 2005, 12ff.; Huczynski 2006, 206ff.; Alvesson 2013, 130ff.; Collins 2020, 135ff.). A way is promised through which

---

69 That pioneer organizations have a larger number of expert interviews, participant observations and document analysis is the great exception. For the method of a follow-up study of such pioneer organizations based on interviews, participant observations, and document analysis, see in detail Kühl 2017.
70 See Bernardis et al. 2017, 8 for an example of the effects of such a "copy and paste" process—for example, the often monotonous reference to the same organizations over and over again, W.L.Gore, Morning Star, Semco, or Valve—sometimes decades after these organizations were once pioneers and without sensitivity to the fact that the principles of success there have not infrequently already been abolished.

the work—and furthermore, life—can become meaningful again. Principles are praised with which one can advance into new levels of consciousness. Prophesies predict catastrophe if you don't commit to these new ideas. Not only the salvation of the individual, but of the whole world is promised.[71]

Critics pick up on the religion-like nature of management fads and complain that it is not uncommon for followers of management concepts to resemble members of a cult. Adherents of a management concept declare themselves to be a group of chosen ones who have grasped how organizations should function today. The application of a management concept, its followers argue, is a "spiritual practice" of which as many others as possible should be convinced (see Holacracy Tincup 2014; Infinite Beta 2018).

What this criticism overlooks, however, is that these quasi-religious management concepts fulfill important functions in organizations. Even if the making of modern management fashions resembles long-established religions in almost surprising ways, with these ardent managers and consultants animated by their own concepts reminding us almost inevitably of the orthodox advocates of a religion, management fashions can play a central role in change processes in organizations.

Management Fashions as Support for Decision-Making

Organizations face the challenge of having to make decisions under conditions of high uncertainty. If the right course of action were clear to everyone, there would ultimately be no need to make a decision, because it would be obvious what has to be done. Decisions are therefore always determinations in a situation in which you cannot be sure whether the decision is correct. Therefore, every decision made in an organization is inevitably risky, because it may turn out later that a different decision would have been better after all (see Luhmann 1993, 287ff.).

---

71 On the religious qualities of Theory U and the resulting blind spots, see Kühl 2020b.

Ultimately, organizations could rely on themselves for decision-making. Organizations usually understand their problems with such precision that they already have the necessary know-how for assessing decision alternatives. There is knowledge in the organizations about where communication problems between departments come from and how they can be dealt with, which routines do not work as they should, and which people are in the right jobs and which are not. So in terms of knowledge alone, organizations should be able to weigh the pros and cons of decision alternatives and make a decision based on their deliberations.

The problem, however, is that the responsibility for this decision then lies solely with the decision-makers within the organization. If it turns out that a decision must be perceived as "wrong" for the organization on balance, then the search for culprits often begins. Staff are identified who made the decision at the time and can therefore be held responsible for it (see Luhmann 1964, 172ff.). While it could be argued that "decision makers" in organizations are well paid because they make decisions under uncertain conditions, there are still good reasons to develop strategies to reject responsibility for a decision if it is later perceived to be wrong.

The strategies for reducing personally attributable responsibility are many and varied. In many cases, the large expert consulting firms are brought in not because of the quality of their consulting services, but because responsibility for decisions can be outsourced to them. The department of collective decision-making bodies in the form of self-organized teams reduces the individual responsibility of each team member. The integration of as many people as possible through participative change processes makes it more difficult to hold individuals solely responsible for a decision.

Given the risks involved in decision-making, management fads play an important role. Managers can justify decisions by saying that all organizations are following a trend at the moment. When redesigning an organization, this is seen as the only way to deal with the changing requirements in the management concepts currently being bandied about. One justifies one's own approach by imitating the structures of those organizations that are discussed in the management press as particularly progressive and are therefore considered particularly successful. In short, management fashions serve as helpful security surrogates in such a situation. They not only reduce the necessity of thinking for yourself, but also help to reduce your own responsibility for decisions.

Holacracy as a Ready-Made Organizational Concept

The charm of, and the problem with, many management fashions is that they consist of a clever mixture of simplicity and ambiguity (Clark and Salaman 1996, 85ff.; Kieser 1997, 58). The simplicity of most management fashions creates the impression of spontaneous plausibility. Firms that let their employees act as entrepreneurs within the company appear more appealing than firms that stifle employee initiative with bureaucratic procedures. A company that follows the model of a tent that can be moved quickly appears more attractive than companies that follow the model of a palace. Organizations that are structured in a network-like manner evoke more sympathy than organizations that are constructed in a centralized manner (all examples in Kieser 1997, 58f.).

But it is precisely this plausible simplicity that leads many management fashions to remain unclear about exactly how they should be implemented (Miller and Hartwick 2002, 26f.; Miller et al. 2004, 12). While the recipe-like presentation of the approach, the examples of pioneering organizations, and the chapters on implementation suggest immediate practicality, they often leave practitioners perplexed (Micklethwait and Wooldrige 1996, 83).[72] Basically, as Alfred Kieser states (1995, 63), management fads are "collections of relatively simple principles." They provide managers with "guiding principles," "simplify" their view of the world, and focus on individual "success factors," but do not provide "exact methods." They buttress the utopia of an orga-

---

72 The ideal type of this is the biggest management bestseller to date, "In Search of Excellence"; see Peters and Waterman 1982.

nization based on trust and awareness, which are in no way suitable as a blueprint for structuring an organization (see Caddell 2016).

Because most management fashions are both simple and clear, yet also ambiguous and vague (Kieser 1996, 25), there is a high degree of uncertainty among decision makers in organizations about how to implement such fads. While a myriad of consultants offer their services in implementing a management fashion, a lack of clarity remains as to exactly what conclusions need to be drawn for the organization. This is precisely where holacracy stands out from many other management fashions.

Unlike most management concepts, holacracy spells out in minute detail how an organization should function. While management concepts such as the learning organization, the agile organization or the intelligent enterprise remain unclear what exactly changes in an organization with the introduction of these concepts, holacratic organizations, similar to Taylorist concepts and the Harzburg model, spell out the principles in detail.

Unlike many other management fashions that have only produced effects on the display side of the organization, holacracy digs deep into the organization's formal structure. The holacratic constitution signed at the start date of a reform process leads to the splitting of tasks into well-defined roles, the grouping of these roles into circles, and the linking of these circles via lead links and rep links. Software systems based on the holacratic constitution enforce the adoption of the highly formalized holacratic interaction formats for the specification of roles.

In holacracy, the *package character* of a management fashion is particularly clear (see on the concept of this package character Gill and Whittle 1992, 282). In management fashions, the various management tools are combined into a package and then given impressive labels such as "total quality management," "lean management," or "holacratic operating system" (on this logic, see Reitzig 2022, 179f.). Management is promised that all they have to do is unpack the package, and then they can immediately start reaping benefits from the management tools (see Huczynski 2006, 112).

The advantage of this packaged approach to management is that a management concept can be purchased in its entirety. Just as you can delete outdated software and replace it with new standard software, you can also delete the organization's old operating system and replace it with a holacratic system; at least that is the sales pitch. As with standard software, you may have to make one or two adjustments to a holacratic system, but in general you know what you are getting. This is an enormous relief in the decision-making process.

However, the disadvantage of such a package is that you are more or less at the mercy of the ready-made solution. Just as you have to develop laborious "workarounds" for the weak points of a new standard software, you also have to find ways to compensate for the unwanted side effects of a new operating system. But these are always stopgap solutions that can merely contain the problems, but not fundamentally solve them. If the difficulties are too great, the only option is often to replace the standard software with new software or to say goodbye to the organizational operating system.

6.3 On the Rise and Decline of a Management Fashion

Management fashions—like fashions in general—are by nature temporary (see Abrahamson 1996, 255). A management fad quickly becomes popular, but remains in the general focus for only a comparatively short time and then increasingly loses its appeal. In many cases, management fashions fade slowly, but sometimes they lose popularity very quickly when the failure of a pioneering organization becomes known and it becomes clear that the promises associated with the fashion are not being fulfilled (Miller, Hartwick et al. 2004, 7).

The success of the holacratic organizational model in management discourse is related to the fact that it was able to anchor itself prominently in the discourse on new agile organizational forms. The gap in the market was the promise of filling the very vague idea of agility with a detailed organizational concept.

Management Fashions under Scrutiny

Management fashions always look good on paper. The representations of the principles look convincing. The promises of effectiveness gains, increased efficiency and innovative power are great. The concepts are then introduced into organizations with high expectations. But the more the concepts are tested in practice, the more obvious their difficulties become. The unintended side effects become more apparent and the assessments of the concept more skeptical. Holacracy inevitably suffered the fate of other early management fads: after a period of strong euphoria and interest, it came under increasing criticism and then slowly lost influence.

The difficulties of management fashions that undergo practical testing do not have to mean that the organizational form imagined as a revolution is less suitable than the previous ones. The old management concepts also attracted criticism because of their side effects. Otherwise, the organization would have had no reason to adopt a current management fashion. But over time, knowledge about the weaknesses of the old organizational form erodes and negative experiences with the new concept come to the fore.

At this point, the advocates of management fashion begin to pay the price for having touted their concept as an organizational panacea. The excess of euphoria in the promotion of the concept inevitably leads to the disappointment of expectations. Critical reports increasingly appear in the mass media, where the concept was initially celebrated. Organizations become increasingly hesitant about experimenting with the concept.

The Difficulties of the Pioneer Organizations

Pioneer organizations that have contributed significantly to the plausibility of a concept play a special role in the decline of a management fashion. In the early days of a management fashion, the vanguard organizations attract a lot of attention. They benefit from their role as a pioneer organization by gaining legitimacy in the public eye, providing free publicity for their products, and enjoying advantages in recruiting employees. Because of this public prominence, however, there is also a great deal of interest in the difficulties of these pioneer organizations. Critical reports from employees who have left are read carefully, the organization's problems are commented on in detail, and the abolition of the management concept in the pioneer organizations is reported on extensively (see Rosenzweig 2014, 33ff.).

The normal mechanisms of the mass media are at work when it comes to pioneering organizations. As with athletes, musicians or politicians, they are hyped up when they achieve their first successes and thus gain prominence. But at the first clear signs of problems, this very prominence becomes a problem for them. While the difficulties of unknown people do not usually attract mass media attention, their prominence makes them newsworthy. Crises are then not reported in the mass media because these crises are interesting per se, but because it is the crisis of a prominent athlete, musician, politician or even an organization. Just as quickly as one is celebrated in the mass media as the embodiment of a new trend, one is also treated as a symbol of its decline.

In view of these difficulties, the managers of pioneer organizations face a dilemma. On the one hand, there are growing indications in the organization that the introduction of the management concept is leading to considerable difficulties. The fading of the management fashion could allow the organization to realign and move away from the management concept. On the other hand, the organization is so strongly associated with a management concept in the public eye that it could mean significant reputational damage if the concept were to be withdrawn.

If management doesn't identify too strongly with holacracy, it can roll back the concept and make the reasons public (on the case at Medium, see Doyle 2016; on the one at Github, see Oane 2016). If management has strongly committed to a management concept, it often takes new management to change that concept again. But even then, it is often not possible to publicly abandon the concept. Instead, central principles are withdrawn, but at the same time management pretends that the concept is still the guideline for action. In holacratic organizations, the highly standardized interaction formats are then abandoned, the circles are replaced by profit centers, and employee performance is measured by the success of these profit centers, but at the same time the organization still presents itself as holacratic (as in the case of Zappos; see Groth 2020).[73]

It is precisely the reports of the difficulties experienced by pioneer organizations that lead to to an increasing loss of reputation for a management fashion. The failure of pioneer organizations makes criticism of the concept plausible, and decision makers in organizations increasingly doubt whether they should take the risk of introducing what for a time was regarded as a panacea.

Immunizations, Declines and Renaissances

Problems with the decline of a management fad arise in particular for consultants who have strongly linked their reputation with it. There is an increasing trend in the consulting scene to no longer support clients in the introduction of decentralized or centralized, hierarchical or de-hierarchicalized, formalized or de-formalized forms of organization, depending on the situation. Instead, consultants present themselves as experts in a precisely defined organizational concept. This leads to high acceptance at the peak of a management fashion, but causes problems at the latest when a management fashion loses its appeal.

As a result, consultants who have specialized in the implementation of an organizational model and have associated their reputations with it are

---

73 Almost all of the original holacratic pioneering organizations have retracted this concept. For the disavowal of the holacratic concept in pioneer organizations such as GitHub and Medium, see Carr 2016 or Oane 2016; on the abandonment of the concept at Blinkist, see Uzun 2021; on the erosion of holacracy at Zappos, see Groth 2020 and Grind and Sayre 2022, 251. The company ternary software, which was the first to adopt holacracy and is repeatedly cited as a role model (for example, in Neal 2013, 173f.), has not only abolished holacracy again, but has ceased to exist altogether (see Groth 2018a). Regarding the transience of management concepts, we need only refer to the disappearance of the Harzburg model from public perception—a management model in which hundreds of thousands of managers were trained in Germany.

responding to growing criticism by escalating their "commitment" (thus Caddell 2016 in reference to Zappos). While there is great willingness to learn among proponents during the peak phase of a management fashion, increasing immunization tendencies set in as decline accelerates. The rejection of a management fad is then explained by the fact that executives cannot cope with the "new understanding of their role" because they are still too attached to an understanding of leadership shaped by the traditional, conformist, modern performance-oriented organization (Kuhlmann and Horn 2020, 218). Critics of the concept are accused of not having experienced the concept in practice themselves, which ostensibly renders them unable to recognize the advantages of the concept, unlike the "mature practitioners" (Wittrock 2021).

Management concepts in which the principles have not been described in detail can still hold their own for a while by integrating new content into the concept. Management fashions such as the "learning organization," the "knowledge-based firm," and the "self-organized enterprise" are so general in nature that various organizational principles, even contradictory ones, can easily be subsumed under them. These very vaguely defined management fashions then disappear not because certain principles have turned out to be unsuitable in the organization in detail, but because they have outlived their usefulness as a label for reforms in an organization.

The tragedy of management concepts whose formal structural foundations are defined down to the last detail is that they can only react to a very limited extent to the side effects that become increasingly apparent in practice, the failure of their pioneer organizations, and the increasingly ferocious criticism of the concept. While it is possible—as in the case of holacracy—to try to bring ever newer versions of the concept to market, fundamental changes to the model are not possible. What then often remains are the euphoric reports about the management concept that have become history, the ruins of failed management reforms in organizations that are often difficult to conceal, and one or two interesting tools that can continue working under new names.

But the decline of a management fashion does not mean that its structural principle disappears for good. Forgetfulness in management discourse means that an organizational structural principle can experience a renaissance after a decade or two. Organizations which, precisely because of the problems of hyperformalization of organizations, rely on extensive deformalization then find that this leads to a whole series of problematic side effects, such as an explosion of internal complexity (see Kühl 2017, 102ff.). This then makes management concepts that try to get a grip on these problems via strong formalization appear attractive again. The idea of hyperformalization then becomes en vogue again, albeit under a new name.

What conclusions can we draw from this rise and fall of management fashions?

6.4 The Alternation Between Praising the Role and Celebrating the Person

In the discussion of new organizational forms, which is shaped by management fashions, there is sometimes an erratic switching back and forth between an emphasis on expectation formation via formal roles and an emphasis on informal expectation formation among the staff. Consultancies that come from a group dynamics tradition in which expectation formation occurs via a strong thematization of personal idiosyncrasies and desires show themselves to be particularly receptive to concepts such as holacracy that focus almost exclusively on roles. Grassroots political organizations, which as they grow run into the limits of expectation formation via knowledge of persons, look to hyperformalized organizational models like holacracy as their salvation.[74] In contrast, organizations that rely on a strong emphasis on roles with

---

74 Interestingly, there is little research on associations and nongovernmental organizations that are holacratic. One reason could be that associations and nongovernmental organizations that rely significantly on the work of volunteers are very quickly confronted with the effects of hyperformalization and therefore abandon holacracy before it could be researched. For the grassroots political organization Extinction Rebellion's consideration of using the holacratic model of organization, see Groth 2019. For the first scientific references, see Smiles and Edwards 2021. On the phenomenon, see also Hensby, Sibthorpe, and Driver 2012.

holacracy then introduce the concept of nonviolent communication in a backlash to improve understanding among people in the organization. Some holacratic organizations that feel stifled by hyperformalization abruptly abolish the hard-won formal rules and, in a fierce counter-reaction, rely on largely person-centered expectation formation.

In some cases, this oscillation back and forth between the extreme pole of expectation formation via people and that of expectation formation via roles can be useful because it keeps the organization moving. Particularly in the discovery phase of an organization, experimenting with extreme variants can provide experience with different forms of structure formation. In other cases, however, it may be functional, instead of relying on extreme variants, to balance exactly how much the organization should prescribe role behavior through its formal structure and how much room it wants to leave for expectation formation via the knowledge of individuals. In doing so, organizations try to determine on a case-by-case basis which formal programs require role behavior independent of staff, and which formalization gaps should be left where good knowledge of people can then be used to create the necessary security of expectation.

But in both approaches, it helps to have a precise understanding of how role and person expectations work. Instead of using ever new formulations, ever more peppy terms and ever more colorful images to celebrate a blanket enthusiasm for staff, only to demand behavior dictated by the formal role again shortly afterwards, it seems more important to get a realistic view of the relationship between role and person in the respective organization. In this context, it may well be that in a start-up equipped with an attractive purpose, or a self-governing company owned by the employees, the significance of the person for the formation of expectations is quite different from that in a hospital focused on process reliability or a large company dependent on standardization.

Methodology Epilogue

As a researcher, when you come across something previously unknown, you ultimately have no choice but to research. This was no different with this book. To be sure, there are some self-representations of hyperformalized organizations, some superficial accounts of "learning journeys" by consultants, and a number of shorter articles in business journals and Internet forums. However, this does not provide deeper insight into the structural effects of this management concept. Listening to a Power Point presentation, taking a short walk through a company's rooms, supplemented by reading an interview with one or two hand-picked members of the organization, only provides a view of the organization's exterior.

In order to even begin to understand the functioning of an organization with a few hundred members, one needs—and in this respect the quality requirements of organizational science and organizational consulting do not differ—at least 10 to 15 interviews, participant observation of at least two or three regular interactions, and a stay of at least two or three days in the organization in order to be able to pick up impressions during break discussions. If the analysis is carried out at different points in time, it is easier to perceive inconsistencies in the descriptions and to bring lines of development into focus. In order to classify your own observations, it makes sense to report your own analysis back to the organization and to include the reactions from the organization as further empirical material in the analysis.

One privilege of working at a university that organizes its teaching in a research-oriented way is that, once you have awakened an interest in knowledge, you do not have to wait until you have been granted the necessary research funds after a few years to be able to carry out the research; you can start the empirical survey directly in formats such as seminar and teaching research. I was fortunate that I was not only able to collect the empirical data for this book with a number of outstanding sociologists at Bielefeld University and at the University of Lucerne, but also to work with them in a series of courses on the theoretical classification of the empirical data collected. Whoever is interested in the detailed results of our investigation is referred to the contributions in our joint anthology (Kühl and Sua-Ngam-Iam 2023).

To my own surprise, despite the prominence of some holacratic organizations in the mass media, empirical access was anything but easy. The originally promised interviews with a consulting firm that both offered an introduction to holacracy and used the principle of holacracy itself for internal structuring, were canceled at short notice due to strongly increased order volume. Backstage, I then learned that the actual reason for the cancellation was a fierce internal conflict about the holacratic organizational model. The more than understandable concern was that an outside perspective—even if only in the form of a series of interviews—could fuel this conflict. Further attempts to gain field access were also unsuccessful.

In order to gain access to empirical sources, I got into the habit of telling practitioners during my presentations about my difficulties in opening up the research field. In an admittedly pointed form, I described the assumption that it is significantly easier to establish field access in state intelligence agencies, military special forces, and criminal rocker clubs than in holacratic organizations. This provocation led practitioners to approach me after the conferences and provide access to three larger holacratic organizations. In addition, there were two smaller holacratic organizations that responded to direct approaches.

In an initial survey phase, we analyzed the five organizations using expert interviews, participant observation and document analysis. This largely took place on site, sometimes at different locations of the companies. Only individual interviews were conducted via video call when the interviewees were not available on site. In a second phase one year later, further interviews were conducted by video call in four of the five organizations in order to be able to assess the organizations over time as well. In some cases, the interviews took place with interviewees from the first phase, and in others with new interviewees. In the five organizations, we conducted a total of 65 interviews with 52 members, preliminary and final interviews with our contacts, and observations of a total of nine meetings (seven tactical meetings and two governance meetings). We made audio recordings of both the interviews and the meetings when possible. Notes were taken of the non-recorded conversations during the interview (for details of the survey, see Sua-Ngam-Iam 2023a).

In our analyses, we have drawn on a method that we have already developed in various research projects on organizational forms: Focusing on vanguard organizations in management discourse. Pioneer organizations are organizations that draw attention to themselves by introducing organizational features that are considered modern and are thus considered role models for organizations in the same organizational field. The case analysis of a vanguard organization contrasts with the methodology of contingency-theoretically oriented organizational research. These usually draw on "typical" companies, administrations, hospitals or universities and aim to match as many variables as possible. In contrast to this approach, however, the analysis of pioneer organizations does not aim to establish a primarily empirically proven thesis through large samples. Rather, the study of vanguard organizations serves to develop considerations and illustrate a theoretically supported argument.

In principle, holacracy can be analyzed in more detail in different types of organizations (see Bischof 2019, 69). First, there are individual departments in large organizations that experiment with holacratic principles. As a rule, these are staff departments from the areas of personnel development, training or communication, which have come into contact with the holacratic principle through their consultants. Second, there are micro-organizations—so-called face-to-face organizations—that are trying to give themselves clearer structures via holacracy. It is not uncommon for these to be smaller consulting firms that advise other organizations on how to implement holacracy. Third, there are organizations that are implementing holacracy at the stage where they would need to bring in a middle management level due to their growth in size and are looking for alternatives to traditional hierarchical forms of structuring. We focused our research on the last type of organization because we felt that the structural effects of holacracy could be observed particularly well there.

Our studies on holacracy are part of a larger research project on the "archaeology" of management fashions. In addition to the holacratic organizational model, our interests are focused on the Harzburg model (for a rather critical discussion of this see Guserl 1973; Grunwald and Bernthal 1983; Müller 2019; Chapoutot 2020) and Business Process Reengineering (see critically Grint 1994; Jackson 1996; Fincham 2000). Although these management programs no longer play a role in practice, it is precisely in retrospect that general insights into the rise and fall of management concepts can be drawn from them.

Bibliography

Abrahamson, Eric. 1996. "Management Fashion." *Academy of Management Review* 21: 254–85.
Adler, Paul S. 1999. "Building Better Bureaucracies." *Academy of Management Perspectives* 13: 36–47.
Adler, Paul S. 2003. "Toward Collaborative Interdependence: A Century of Change in the Organization of Work." In *Industrial Relations to Human Resources and Beyond: The Evolving Process of Employee Relations Management*, edited by Bruce E. Kaufman, Richard A. Beaumont, and Roy B. Helfgott, 353–99. Armonk: M.E. Sharpe.
Adler, Paul S., and Charles Heckscher. 2006. "Towards Collaborative Community." In *The Firm as a Collaborative Community: Reconstructing Trust in the Knowledge Economy*, edited by Paul Adler, 11–105. Oxford: Oxford University Press.
Aghion, Philippe, and Jean Tirole. 1997. "Formal and Real Authority in Organizations." *Journal of Political Economy* 105: 1–29.
Alexy, Oliver. 2022. "How Flat Can It Get? From Better at Flatter to the Promise of the Decentralized, Boundaryless Organization." *Journal of Organization Design* 11: 31–36.
Allen, David. 2001. *Getting Things Done: The Art of Stress-Free Productivity*. New York: Penguin Books.
Alvesson, Mats. 2013. *The Triumph of Emptiness: Consumption, Higher Education, and Work Organization*. Oxford/ New York: Oxford University Press.
Alvesson, Mats, and Paul Thompson. 2005. "Post-Bureaucracy?" In *The Oxford Handbook of Work and Organization*, edited by Stephen Ackroyd, Rosemary Batt, Thompson, Paul, and Pamela S. Tolbert, 485–507. Oxford: Oxford University Press.
Anders, George. 2014. "Gurus Gone Wild: Does Zappos' Reorganization Make Any Sense." https://www.forbes.com/sites/georgeanders/2014/01/09/gurus-gone-wild-does-zappos-reorganization-make-any-sense/#6c48b1c331ae.

Aoki, Masahiko. 1990. *Information, Incentives, and Bargaining in the Japanese Economy.* Cambridge: Cambridge University Press.

Appelo, Jurgen. 2016. "Holacracy Is Fundamentally Broken." https://www.forbes.com/sites/jurgenappelo/2016/07/14/holacracy-is-fundamentally-broken/#1771bda21126.

Ashkenas, Ron, Dave Ulrich, Tood Jick, and Steve Kerr. 1995. *The Boundaryless Organization: Breaking the Chains of Organizational Structure.* San Francisco: Jossey-Bass.

Aspers, Patrik. 2005. *Markets in Fashion: A Phenomenological Approach.* London: Routledge.

Barker, James R. 1993. "Tightening the Iron Cage: Convertive Control in Self Managing Teams." *Administrative Science Quarterly* 38: 408–37.

Barnard, Chester I. 1938. *The Functions of the Executive.* Cambridge: Harvard University Press.

Barrett, Richard. 2013. *Liberating the Corporate Soul.* Hoboken: Taylor and Francis.

Beck, Kent, Mike Beedle, Arie van Bennekum, Alistair Cockburn, Ward Cunningham, Martin Fowler, James Grenning et al. 2001. "Manifesto for Agile Software Development." https://agilemanifesto.org/.

Benefiel, Margaret. 2005. *Soul at Work: Spiritual Leadership in Organizations.* La Vergne: Church Publishing Incorporated. https://ebookcentral.proquest.com/lib/kxp/detail.action?docID=6793134.

Bernardis, Alexander, Gerhard Hochreiter, Matthias Lang, and Gerald Mitterer. 2017. "Auf zu Neuen Ufern." *Harvard Business Manager Edition* (4): 6–12.

Bernoux, Philippe. 1985. *La Sociologie Des Organisations.* Paris: Seuil.

Bernstein, Ehtan, John Bunch, Niko Canner, and Michael Lee. 2016. "Beyond the Holacracy Hype." *Harvard Business Review* (6): 38–49.

Bernstein, Ethan S. 2012. "The Transparency Paradox: A Role for Privacy in Organizational Learning and Operational Control." *Administrative Science Quarterly* 57 (2): 181–216.

Bischof, Nicole. 2019. "Self-Leadership in selbstorganisierten Systemen am Beispiel Holacracy." In *Führen in der Arbeitswelt 4.0*, edited by Christoph Negri, 63–72. Berlin/Heidelberg: Springer.

Blau, Peter M. 1954. "Co-Operation and Competition in a Bureaucracy." *American Journal of Sociology* 59: 530–35.
Blau, Peter M. 1956. *Bureaucracy in Modern Society.* New York: Random House.
Blau, Peter M., and Marshall W. Meyer. 1971. *Bureaucracy in Modern Society.* New York: Random House.
Block, Peter. 2013. *Stewardship: Choosing Service over Self-Interest.* 2nd ed. Oakland: Berrett-Koehler Publishers. https://ebookcentral.proquest.com/lib/kxp/detail.action?docID=1172489.
Bottani, Eleonora. 2010. "Profile and Enablers of Agile Companies: An Empirical Investigation." *International Journal of Production Economics* 125 (2): 251–61. https://doi.org/10.1016/j.ijpe.2010.02.016.
Braverman, Harry. 1974. *Labor and Monopoly Capital: The Degradation of Work in the Twentieth Century.* New York/ London: Monthly Review Press.
Brodda, Dustin. 2023. "Führen ohne Weisungshierarchie: Über die Informale Kompensation hierarchischer Kontrolle in holakratischen Organisationen." In *Holacracy: Funktionen und Folgen eines Managementmodells*, edited by Stefan Kühl, and Sua-Ngam-Iam, Wiesbaden: Springer Gabler.
Bruch, Heike, and Stefan Berger. 2016. "Leadership wird noch wichtiger! Vier Hebel der Modernisierung von Führung." *Personalführung* (6): 18–23.
Burns, Tom, and George M. Stalker. 1961. *The Management of Innovation.* London: Tavistock.
Caddell, Bud. 2016. "The Fatal Gap Between Organizational Theory and Organizational Practice." https://medium.nobl.io/the-fatal-gap-between-organizational-theory-and-organizational-practice-ccaea23d0815.
Cafferata, Gail Lee. 1982. "The Building of Democratic Organizations: An Embryological Metaphor." *Administrative Science Quarterly* 27: 280–303.
Campbell, Andrew, and Michael Goold. 2000. *The Collaborative Enterprise: Why Links Across the Corporation Often Fail and Jow to Make Them Work.* Cambridge: Perseus Books.

Carr, Paul Bradley. 2015a. "A Holacracy of Dunces." https://pandodaily.com/2015/07/03/holacracy-dunces.
Carr, Paul Bradley. 2015b. "Astonishingly, Tony Hsieh's Holacracy Experiment Is Causing Chaos at Zappos." https://pandodaily.com/2015/10/07/astonishingly-tony-hsiehs-holacracy-experiment-causing-chaos-zappos.
Carr, Paul Bradley. 2016. "Medium Drops Holacracy, Because Holacracy Is "Time-Consuming and Divisive"." https://pandodaily.com/2016/03/07/medium-drops-holacracy-because-holacracy-time-consuming-and-divisive.
Carson, Paula Phillips, Patricia A. Lanier, Kerry David Carson, and Brandi N. Guidry. 2000. "Clearing a Path Through the Management Fashion Jungle: Some Preliminary Trailbazing." *Academy of Management Journal* 43 (6): 1143–58. https://doi.org/10.2307/1556342.
Chapoutot, Johann. 2020. *Libres D'obéir: Le Management, Du Nazisme À Aujourd'hui.* Paris: Gallimard.
Ciborra, Claudio. 1996. "The Platform Organization: Recombining Strategies, Structures, and Surprises." *Organization Science* 7: 103–18.
Clark, Timothy, and David Greatbatch. 2016. "Management Fashion as Image-Spectacle." *Management Communication Quarterly* 17 (3): 396–424. https://doi.org/10.1177/0893318903257979.
Clark, Timothy, and Graeme Salaman. 1996. "The Management Guru as Organizational Witchdoctor." *Organization* 3: 85–107.
Cohen, Harry. 1965. *The Denomics of Bureaucracy.* Iowa: Iowa State University Press.
Collins, David. 2020. *Management Gurus: A Research Overview.* London/ New York: Routledge.
Collins, James C. 2001. *Good to Great: Why Some Companies Make the Leap ... And Others Don't.* New York: HarperBusiness.
Constas, Helen. 1958. "Max Weber's Two Conceptions of Bureaucracy." *American Journal of Sociology* 63: 400–409.
Coulson-Thomas, Colin, and Richard Brown. 1989. *The Responsive Organisation: People Management : The Challenge of the 1990s.* Corby: British Institute of Management Foundation.

Cowan, Chris. 2017. "Holacracy® Basics: How to Make Sure Someone Does Something." https://blog.holacracy.org/how-to-make-sure-someone-does-something-in-holacracy-b84c847c614e.
Cronin, Matthew A. 2015. "Advancing the Science of Dynamics in Groups and Teams." *Organizational Psychology Review* 5: 267–69.
Crozier, Michel. 1963. *Le phénomène bureaucratique.* Paris: Seuil.
Crozier, Michel. 1989. *L'entreprise à l'écoute: Apprendre le management postindustriel.* Paris: Interéditions.
Cyert, Richard M., and James G. March. 1963. *A Behavorial Theory of the Firm.* Englewood Cliffs: Prentice-Hall.
Dalton, Melville. 1959. *Men Who Manage.* New York: Wiley.
Denning, Steve. 2014. "Making Sense of Zappos and Holacracy." https://www.forbes.com/sites/stevedenning/2014/01/15/making-sense-of-zappos-and-holacracy/.
Diefenbach, Thomas, and John A.A. Sillince. 2011. "Formal and Informal Hierarchy in Different Types of Organization." *Organization Studies* 32 (11): 1515–37. https://doi.org/10.1177/0170840611421254.
DiMaggio, Paul J. 2001. "Introduction: Making Sense of the Contemporary Firm and Prefiguring Its Future." In *The Twenty First Century Firm: Changing Economic Organization in International Perspective*, edited by Paul J. DiMaggio, 3–30. Princeton/ Oxford: Princeton University Press.
DiMaggio, Paul J., and Walter W. Powell. 1983. "The Iron Cage Revisited: Institutional Isomorphism and Collective Rationality in Organizational Fields." *American Sociological Review* 48: 147–60.
Dollase, Rainer. 2011. *Sinn und Unsinn des Qualitätsmanagements: Analyse und Verbesserung.* Berlin: Konrad Adenauer Stiftung.
Donaldson, Lex. 2001. *The Contingency Theory of Organizations.* Thousand Oaks: Sage.
Donnellon, Anne, and Maureen Scullay. 1994. "Teams, Performance, and Rewards: Will the Post Bureaucratic Organization Be a Post Meritocratic Organization?" In *The Post-Bureaucratic Organization: New Perspectives on Organizational Change*, edited by Heckscher Charles, and Donnellon Anne, 63–90. Thousand Oaks: Sage.

Doyle, Andy. 2016. "Management and Organization at Medium." https://blog.medium.com/management-and-organization-at-medium-2228cc9d93e9.

Drucker, Peter F. 2016. *People and Performance: The Best of Peter Drucker on Management*. London: Taylor & Francis.

Eckstein, Bernd, and Judith Muster. 2021. "Postbürokratie und die Agile Unsicherheitsabsorption in Interaktionen." *Gruppe. Interaktion. Organisation. Zeitschrift für Angewandte Organisationspsychologie* 52: 649–57.

Eden, Sören, and Torben Möbius. 2020. "Der Ort der "Betriebsgemeinschaft" in der deutschen Gesellschaft 1933–1945: Neue Perspektiven auf die nationalsozialistische "Ordnung der Arbeit"." In *Industrielle Arbeitswelt und Nationalsozialismus: Der Betrieb als Laboratorium der "Volksgemeinschaft" 1920-1960*, edited by Frank Becker and Daniel Schmidt, 28–60. Essen: Klartext.

Edwards, Richard C. 1979. *Contested Terrain*. New York: Basic Books.

Ehrlich, Howard J. 1977. *Anarchism and Formal Organizations*. Baltimore: Vacant Lots Press.

Eisenstadt, Shmuel N. 1958. "Bureaucracy and Bureaucratization." *Current Sociology* 7: 99–164.

Eisenstadt, Shmuel N. 1959. "Bureaucracy, Bureaucratization, and Debureaucratization." *Administrative Science Quarterly* 4: 302–20.

Emerson, Harrington. 1924. *The Twelve Principles of Efficiency*. New York: The Engineering Magazine.

Endenburg, Gerard. 1988. "Business Without Owners: A Model of Sociocracy." In *From Organization*, edited by R. Benson, 149–52.

Endenburg, Gerard, and Clive Bowden. 1988. *Sociocracy: The Organisation of Decision Making*. Rotterdam: Stichting Sociocratisch Centrum.

Fincham, Robin. 2000. "Management as Magic: Reengineering and the Search for Business Salvation." In *The Reengineering Revolution?: Critical Studies of Corporate Change*, edited by David Knights and Huge Willmott, 174–91. Sage Publications.

Fink, Franziska, and Michael Moeller. 2018. *Purpose Driven Organizations: Sinn – Selbstorganisation – Agilität*. Stuttgart: Schäffer-Poeschel.

Fölsing, Albrecht. 2013. *Albert Einstein: Eine Biographie*. 5.th ed. Frankfurt a.M. Suhrkamp.
Friedrichs, Jürgen. 1968. *Werte und soziales Handeln*. Tübingen: J.C.B. Mohr.
Fuchs, Jürgen. 1992. "Das Unternehmen lebender Organismus oder tote Institution." In *Das biokybernetische Modell*, edited by Jürgen Fuchs, 13–74. Wiesbaden: Gabler.
Fulmer, William E. 2000. *Shaping the Adaptive Organization*. New York: AMACOM.
Furnham, Adrian. 2004. *Management and Myths*. London: Palgrave Macmillan UK.
Gill, John, and Sue Whittle. 1992. "Management by Panacea: Accounting for Transience." *Journal of Management Studies* 30:281–95. https://doi.org/10.1111/j.1467-6486.1993.tb00305.x.
Gouldner, Alvin W. 1954. *Patterns of Industrial Bureaucracy*. Glencoe: Free Press.
Goyk, Rüdiger, and Sven Grote. 2018. "Holakratie - Ein neuer Stern am Himmel der Organisationsentwicklung?" In *Führungsinstrumente aus dem Silicon Valley: Konzepte und Kompetenzen*, edited by Sven Grote and Rüdiger Goyk, 17–35. Berlin: Springer Gabler.
Graeber, David. 2015. *The Utopia of Rules: On Technology, Stupidity, and the Secret Joys of Bureaucracy*. Brooklyn/ London: Melville House.
Greatbatch, David, and Timothy Clark. 2005. *Management Speak: Why We Listen to What Management Gurus Tell Us*. Online-Ausg. London: Routledge.
Grey, Chris, and Christina Garsten. 2001. "Trust, Control and Post-Bureaucracy." *Organization Studies* 22 (2): 229–50.
Grey, Christopher. 2013. *A Very Short, Fairly Interesting and Reasonably Cheap Book About Studying Organizations*. 3rd ed. London, Thousand Oaks/ New Delhi/ Singapore: Sage.
Grind, Kirsten, and Katherine Sayre. 2022. *Happy at Any Cost: The Revolutionary Vision and Fatal Quest of Zappos CEO Tony Hsieh*. New York: Simon & Schuster.
Grint, Keith. 1994. "Reengineering History: Social Resonances and Business Process Reengineering." *Organization* 1: 179–201.

Groth, Aimee. 2013. "Zappos Is Going Holacratic: No Job, No Titles, No Managers." https://qz.com/161210/zappos-is-going-holacratic-no-job-titles-no-managers-no-hierarchy/.

Groth, Aimee. 2015a. "Internal Memo: Zappos Is Offering Severance to Employees Who Aren't All in with Holacracy." https://qz.com/370616/internal-memo-zappos-is-offering-severance-to-employees-who-arent-all-in-with-holacracy/.

Groth, Aimee. 2015b. "Zappos Only Lost 7% of Its Managers in Its Recent Employee Exodus." https://qz.com/423197/zappos-only-lost-7-of-its-managers-in-its-recent-employee-exodus/.

Groth, Aimee. 2016. "Zappos Has Now Lost 18% of Its Employees to Its Radical Buyout Offer." https://qz.com/590632/zappos-has-now-lost-18-of-its-employees-to-its-radical-buyout-offer/.

Groth, Aimee. 2018a. "Is Holacracy the Future of Work or a Management Cult?" https://qz.com/work/1397516/is-holacracy-the-future-of-work-or-a-management-cult/.

Groth, Aimee. 2018b. *The Kingdom of Happiness: Inside Toney Hsieh's Zapponian Utopia*. New York: Touchstone.

Groth, Aimee. 2019. "Extinction Rebellion Is Using Holacracy to Scale Its International Movement." https://qz.com/work/1776861/extinction-rebellion-is-using-holacracy-to-scale-its-international-movement/.

Groth, Aimee. 2020. "Zappos Has Quietly Backed Away from Holacracy." https://qz.com/work/1776841/zappos-has-quietly-backed-away-from-holacracy/.

Grunwald, Wolfgang, and Wilmar F. Bernthal. 1983. "Controversy in German Management: The Harzburg Model Experience." *The Academy of Management Review* 8: 233–41.

Gunasekaran, A. 1998. "Agile Manufacturing: Enablers and an Implementation Framework." *International Journal of Production Research* 36: 1223–47.

Guserl, Richard. 1973. *Das Harzburger Modell*. Wiesbaden: Gabler.

Hackman, J. Richard. 1987. "The Design of Work Teams." In *Handbook of Organizational Behavior*, edited by Jay W. Lorsch, 315–42. New York: Prentice Hall.

Hall, Richard H. 1962. "Intraorganizational and Structural Variation: Application of the Bureaucratic Model." *Administrative Science Quarterly* 17: 295–308.
Hamel, Gary. 2007. *The Future of Management*. Boston: Harvard Business Review Press.
Hamel, Gary. 2011. "First, Let's Fire All the Managers." *Harvard Business Review* 89 (12): 48–60.
Hamel, Gary, and Michele Zanini. 2020. *Humanocracy: Creating Organizations as Amazing as the People Inside Them*. Boston Massachusetts: Harvard Business Review Press.
Hammer, Michael, and James Champy. 1993. *Reengineering the Corporation: A Manifesto for Business Revolution*. New York: HarperBusiness.
Harris, Martin, Louise Briand, and Guy Bellemare. 2006. "A Structurationist Analysis of Post-Bureaucracy in Modernity and Late Modernity." *Journal of Organizational Change Management* 19: 65–79.
Hart, Oliver. 2009. *Firms, Contracts, and Financial Structure*. Oxford: Clarendon Press.
Hasenzagl, Rupert. 2019. "Agile Transformation? Wie kann die Tiefgehende Veränderung bewältigt werden." *Austrian Management Review* 9: 89–101.
Hasenzagl, Rupert. 2020. *Management als Profession: Denkanstöße für die Unternehmensführung*. Stuttgart: Schäffer-Poeschel.
Hasenzagl, Rupert, and Barbara Müller. 2020. "Organisationen ohne Hierarchie? Reflexionen über aktuelle Entwicklungen in der Organisationspraxis." *Austrian Management Review* 10: 11–24.
Hastings, Reed, and Erin Meyer. 2020. *No Rules Rules: Netflix and the Culture of Reinvention*. London: Virgin Books.
Hayek, Friedrich A. von. 1960. *The Constitution of Liberty*. Chicago: University of Chicago Press.
Heckscher, Charles. 1994. "Defining the Post-Bureaucratic Type." In *The Post-Bureaucratic Organization: New Perspectives on Organizational Change*, edited by Charles Heckscher, and Anne Donnellon, 14–62. Thousand Oaks: Sage.
Heckscher, Charles, and Anne Donnellon, eds. 1994. *The Post Bureacratic Organization: New Perspectives on Organizational Change*.

Thousand Oaks: Sage.

Hensby, Alexander, Joanne Sibthorpe, and Stephen Driver. 2012. "Resisting the 'Protest Business': Bureaucracy, Post-Bureaucracy and Active Membership in Social Movement Organizations." *Organization* 19: 809–23.

Hermann, Silke, and Niels Pfläging. 2020. *OpenSpace Beta: Das Handbuch für organisationale Transformation in nur 90 Tagen*. München: Vahlen.

Heydebrand, Wolf. 1989. "New Organizational Forms." *Work and Occupation* 16: 323–57.

Heydebrand, Wolf. 2013. "Postbureaucratic Organizations." In *Sociology of Work: An Encyclopedia*, edited by Vicki Smith, 689–93. Los Angeles/ London/ New Delhi: Sage.

Hilbert, Richard A. 1987. "Bureaucracy as Belief, Rationalization as Repair: Max Weber in a Functionalist Age." *Sociological Theory* 5: 70–86.

Hock, Dee. 2005. *One from Many: VISA and the Rise of the Chaordic Organization*. San Francisco/ Berkeley: Berrett-Koehler. https://search.ebscohost.com/login.aspx?direct=true&scope=site&db=nlebk&db=nlabk&AN=260699.

Hodge, Roger D. 2015. "First, Let's Get Rid of All the Bosses." https://newrepublic.com/article/122965/can-billion-dollar-corporation-zappos-be-self-organized.

Hodgson, Damian E. 2004. "Project Work: The Legacy of Bureaucratic Control in the Post-Bureaucratic Organization." *Organization* 11: 81–100.

Hofstede, Geert. 1980. *Culture's Consequences: International Differences in Work Related Values*. Beverly Hills/ London: Sage.

Höhn, Reinhard. 1966. *Führungsbrevier der Wirtschaft*. Bad Harzburg: Verlag für Wissenschaft, Wirtschaft und Technik.

Höhn, Reinhard. 1969. *Führungsbrevier der Wirtschaft*. 6th ed. Bad Harzburg: Verlag für Wissenschaft, Wirtschaft und Technik.

Höhn, Reinhard. 1978. *Das tägliche Brot des Managers*. Bad Harzburg: wwt.

Höhn, Reinhard. 1986. *Die innere Kündigung im Unternehmen*. Bad Harzburg: wwt.

HolacracyOne. 2013. *Holacracy Constituion: Version 4.1.* Houston: Holacryone.
HolacracyOne. 2015. *Holacracy Verfassung: Version 4.1.De.* Wien: dwarfandgiants.org.
HolacracyOne. 2020. *Holacracy Constitution 5.0.* Houston: Holacracyone.
Hood, Christopher. 2007. "What Happens When Transparency Meets Blame-Avoidance?" *Public Management Review* 9: 191–210.
Höpfl, Harro M. 2006. "Post-bureaucracy and Weber's "Modern" Bureaucrat." *Journal of Organizational Change Management* 19:8–21. https://doi.org/10.1108/09534810610643659.
Horch, Heinz-Dieter. 1983. *Strukturbesonderheiten freiwilliger Vereinigungen: Analyse und Untersuchung einer alternativen Form menschlichen Zusammenarbeitens.* Frankfurt a.M./ New York: Campus.
Hsieh, Tony. 2010. *Delivering Happiness: A Path to Profits, Passion, and Purpose.* First edition. New York/ Boston: Grand Central Publishing.
Huczynski, Andrzej. 2006. *Management Gurus: What Makes Them and How to Become One.* 2nd ed. London: Routledge.
Infinite Beta. 2018. "How Holacracy Is Killing Businesses." https://medium.com/infinitebeta/how-holacracy-is-killing-businesses-a425fd0b7eb4.
Jackson, Bradley G. 1996. "Re-Engineering the Sense of Self: The Manager and the Management Guru." *Journal of Management Studies* 33: 571–90.
Jaques, Elliott. 1951. *The Changing Culture of a Factory.* New York: Dryden. https://ebookcentral.proquest.com/lib/kxp/detail.action?docID=1273118.
Jaques, Elliott. 1989. *Requisite Organization: The CEO's Guide to Creative Structure & Leadership.* Gloucester: Cason Hall.
Jones, Gareth R. 1984. "Task Visibility, Free Riding, and Shirking: Explaining the Effect of Structure and Technology on Employee Behavior." *Academy of Management Review* 9: 684–95.
Josserand, Emmanuel, Stephen Teo, and Stewart Clegg. 2006. "From Bureaucratic to Post-bureaucratic: The Difficulties of Transition."

Journal of Organizational Change Management 19:54–64. https://doi.org/10.1108/09534810610643686.

Kanter, Rosabeth Moss. 1983. *The Change Master: Innovation for Productivity in the American Corporation.* New York: Simon & Schuster.

Kates, Amy, Greg Kesler, and Michele DiMartino. 2021. *Networked, Scaled, and Agile: A Design Strategy for Complex Organizations.* London/ New York/ New Delhi: KoganPage.

Kaube, Jürgen. 2020. *Hegels Welt.* Berlin: Rowohlt.

Kaufmann, Jean-Claude. 1996. *Frauenkörper - Männerblicke: Soziologie Des Oben-Ohne.* Konstanz: UVK.

Kellogg, Katherine C., Wanda J. Orlikowski, and Joanne Yates. 2006. "Life in the Trading Zone: Structuring Coordination Across Boundaries in Postbureaucratic Organizations." *Organization Science* 17 (1): 22–44. https://doi.org/10.1287/orsc.1050.0157.

Kette, Sven. 2021. "Das Problem Der Initiative: Funktionen und Folgen eines postbürokratischen Imperativs." In *Postbürokratisches Organisieren: Formen und Folgen agiler Arbeitsweisen*, edited by Judith Muster, Finn-Rasmus Bull, and Jens Kapitzky, 125–43. München: Vahlen.

Kieser, Alfred. 1995. "Managementlehre und Taylorismus." In *Organisationstheorien*, edited by Alfred Kieser. 2nd ed., 57–90. Stuttgart/ Köln/ Berlin: Kohlhammer.

Kieser, Alfred. 1996. "Moden & Mythen des Organisierens." *Die Betriebswirtschaft* 56: 21–39.

Kieser, Alfred. 1997. "Rhetoric and Myth in Management Fashion." *Organization* 4: 49–74.

Knights, David, and Hugh Willmott, eds. 2000. *The Reengineering Revolution? Critical Studies of Corporate Change.* London/ Thousand Oaks/ New Delhi: Sage.

Knights, David, and Hugh Willmott. 2000. "The Reengineering Revolution? An Introduction." In *The Reengineering Revolution?: Critical Studies of Corporate Change*, edited by David Knights and Huge Willmott , 1–25. London/ Thousand Oaks/ New Delhi: Sage.

Koestler, Arthur. 1967. *The Ghost in the Machine.* London: Hutchinson.

Kofman, Fred. 2006. *Conscious Business: How to Build Value Through Values.* Boulder: Sounds True.

Kotter, John P. 2014. *Accelerate: Building Strategic Agility for a Faster-Moving World*. Boston: Harvard Business Review Press. https://ebookcentral.proquest.com/lib/gbv/detail.action?docID=5182588.

Krell, Gertraude. 1991. "Organisationskultur - Renaissance Der Betriebsgemeinschaft." In *Organisationskultur*, edited by Eberhard Dülfer, 147–60. Stuttgart: Schäffer-Poeschel.

Krell, Gertraude. 1994. *Vergemeinschaftende Personalpolitik: Normative Personallehren, Werksgemeinschaft, NS Betriebsgemeinschaft, Betriebliche Partnerschaft, Japan, Unternehmenskultur*. München/ Mering: Rainer Hampp Verlag.

Kühl, Stefan. 2013. *Organizations: A Systems Approach*. Farnham: Gower.

Kühl, Stefan. 2017. *When the Monkeys Run the Zoo: The Pitfalls of Flat Hierarchies*. Princeton/ Hamburg/ Shanghai/ Singapore/ Versailles/ Zurich: Organizational Dialogue Press.

Kühl, Stefan. 2019a. *The Rainmaker Effect: Contradictions of the Learning Organization*. Princeton/ Hamburg/ Shanghai/ Singapore/ Versailles/ Zurich: Organizational Dialogue Press.

Kühl, Stefan. 2019b. *Work: Marxist and Systems-Theoretical Approaches*. London/ New York: Routledge.

Kühl, Stefan. 2020a. *Sisyphus in Management: The Futile Search for the Optimal Organizational Structure*. Princeton/ Hamburg/ Shanghai/ Singapore/ Versailles/ Zurich: Organizational Dialogue Press.

Kühl, Stefan. 2020b. "The Blind Spots in Theory U: The Reconstruction of a (Change-) Management Fashion." *Journal of Change Management* 20 (4): 314–21. https://doi.org/10.1080/14697017.2020.1744883.

Kühl, Stefan. 2022. *Useful Illegality: The Benefits of Breaking the Rules in Organizations*. Princeton/ Hamburg/ Shanghai/ Singapore/ Versailles/ Zurich: Organizational Dialogue Press.

Kühl, Stefan. 2023. "Schattenstrukturen: Zur Ausbildung Informale Strukturen in Holakratischen Unternehmen." In *Holacracy: Funktionen und Folgen eines Managementmodells*, edited by Stefan Kühl, and Sua-Ngam-Iam, Wiesbaden: Springer Gabler.

Kühl, Stefan, and Phanmika Sua-Ngam-Iam, eds. 2023. *Holacracy: Funktionen und Folgen eines Managementmodells*. Wiesbaden: Springer Gabler.

Kuhlmann, Heike, and Sandra Horn. 2020. *Integrale Führung: Wie Sie mit neuen Ansätzen sich selbst, Teams und Unternehmen entwickeln.* 2nd ed. Wiesbaden: Springer Gabler.

Kumar, Vijay, and Subhasree Mukherjee. 2018. "Holacracy—the Future of Organizing? The Case of Zappos." *Human Resource Management International Digest* 26 (7): 12–15. https://doi.org/10.1108/HRMID-08-2018-0161.

Laloux, Frederic. 2014. *Reinventing Organizations: A Guide to Creating Organizations Inspired by the Next Stage of Human Consciousness.* Brussels: Nelson Parker.

Laloux, Frederic. 2015. *Reinventing Organizations: Ein Leifaden Zur Gestaltung Sinnstiftender Formen Der Zusammenarbeit.* München: Vahlen.

Landier, Hubert. 1987. *L'entreprise Polycellulaire: Pour Penser L'entreprise De Demain.* Paris: Éditions Entreprise moderne.

Landier, Hubert. 1991. *Vers l'entreprise intelligente: Dynamique du changement et mutation du management.* Paris: Calmann Lévy.

Langfred, Claus W. 2000. "The Paradox of Self-Management: Individual and Group Autonomy in Work Groups." *Journal of Organizational Behavior* 21 (5): 563–85. https://doi.org/10.1002/1099-1379(200008)21:5<563:AID-JOB31>3.0.CO;2-H.

Larner, Justin, and Chris Mason. 2014. "Beyond Box-Ticking: A Study of Stakeholder Involvement in Social Enterprise Governance." *Corporate Governance* 14 (2): 181–96. https://doi.org/10.1108/CG-06-2011-0050.

Lawrence, Paul R., and Jay W. Lorsch. 1967. *Organization and Environment: Managing Differentiation and Integration.* Homewood: Irwin.

Lee, Michael Y., and Amy C. Edmondson. 2017. "Self-Managing Organizations: Exploring the Limits of Less-Hierarchical Organizing." *Research in Organizational Behavior* 37:35–58. https://doi.org/10.1016/j.riob.2017.10.002.

Levi, Daniel. 2017. *Group Dynamics for Teams.* 5th ed. Los Angeles: Sage.

Levinthal, Daniel A., and James G. March. 1993. "The Myopia of Learning." *Stragegic Management Journal* 14: 95–112.

Levitt, Barbara, and James G. March. 1988. "Organizational Learning." *Annual Review of Sociology* 14: 319–40.
Likert, Rensis. 1961. *New Patterns of Management*. New York/ Toronto, London.
Likert, Rensis. 1967. *The Human Organisation: Its Management and Value*. New York: McGraw-Hill.
Likert, Rensis, and Charles T. Araki. 1986. "Managing Without a Boss: System 5." *Leadership and Organization Development Journal* 7: 17–20.
Linke, Lars-Peter. 2016. "Holacracy Purpose: Damit alles in Bester Absicht geschieht." https://www.hernstein.at/newsroom/blog/purpose-damit-alles-in-bester-absicht-geschieht/.
Littler, Craig R. 1982. *The Development of the Labour Process in Capitalist Societies: A Comparative Study of Transformation of Work in Britain, Japan and the USA*. London: Heinemann.
Littler, Craig R. 1990. "The Labour Process Debate. A Theoretical Review 1974-1988." In *Labour Process Theory*, edited by David Knights and Hugh Willmott, 46–94. London: Macmillan.
Littler, Craig R., and Graeme Salaman. 1982. "Bravermania and Beyond: Recent Theories of the Labour Process." *Sociology* 16: 251–69.
Luhmann, Niklas. 1964. *Funktionen und Folgen formaler Organisation*. Berlin: Duncker & Humblot.
Luhmann, Niklas. 1965. "Spontane Ordnungsbildung." In *Verwaltung*, edited by Fritz Morstein Marx, 163–83. Berlin: Duncker & Humblot.
Luhmann, Niklas. 1971. "Reform des öffentlichen Dienstes." In *Politische Planung*, edited by Niklas Luhmann, 203–56. Opladen: WDV.
Luhmann, Niklas. 1973. *Zweckbegriff und Systemrationalität*. Frankfurt a.M. Suhrkamp.
Luhmann, Niklas. 1979. *Trust and Power: Two Works*. Chichester/ New York: Wiley.
Luhmann, Niklas. 1981. *Politische Theorie Im Wohlfahrtsstaat*. München/ Wien: Olzog.

Luhmann, Niklas. 1985. *A Sociological Theory of Law*. London: Routledge.
Luhmann, Niklas. 1988. "Organisation." In *Mikropolitik: Rationalität, Macht und Spiele in Organisationen*, edited by Willi Küpper and Günther Ortmann, 165–86. Opladen: WDV.
Luhmann, Niklas. 1993. "Die Paradoxie des Entscheidens." *Verwaltungsarchiv* 84: 287–310.
Luhmann, Niklas. 1995. *Social Systems*. Stanford: Stanford University Press.
Luhmann, Niklas. 2018. *Organization and Decision*. Cambridge: Cambridge University Press.
Mackey, John. 2013. *Conscious Capitalism: Liberating the Heroic Spirit of Business*. Boston: Harvard Business Review Press. https://ebookcentral.proquest.com/lib/kxp/detail.action?docID=5181536.
Manson, Mark. 2020. "The Rise and Fall of Ken Wilber." https://markmanson.net/ken-wilber.
Manz, Charles C., and Henry P. Sims. 1980. "Self Management as a Substitute for Leadership: A Social Learning Theory Perspective." *Academy of Management Review* 5: 361–67.
Manz, Charles C., and Henry P. Sims. 1984. "Searching for the "Unleader": Organizational Member Views on Leading Self Managed Groups." *Human Relations* 37: 409–24.
Manz, Charles C., and Henry P. Sims. 1987. "Leading Workers to Lead Themselves: The External Leadership of Self Managing Work Teams." *Administrative Science Quarterly* 32: 106–28.
Maravelias, Christian. 2003. "Post-bureaucracy—Control Through Professional Freedom." *Journal of Organizational Change Management* 16:547–66. https://doi.org/10.1108/09534810310494937.
March, James G. 2016. *Zwei Seiten Der Erfahrung: Wie Organisationen Intelligenter werden können*. Heidelberg: Carl-Auer.
March, James G., and Johan P. Olsen. 1975. "The Uncertainty of the Past: Organizational Learning Under Ambiguity." *European Journal of Political Research* 3: 147–71.
Martela, Frank. 2019. "What Makes Self-Managing Organizations Novel? Comparing How Weberian Bureaucracy, Mintzberg's

Adhocracy, and Self-Organizing Solve Six Fundamental Problems of Organizing." *Journal of Organization Design* 8:1–23. https://doi.org/10.1186/s41469-019-0062-9.

Matthiesen, Kai, Judith Muster, and Peter Laudenbach. 2022. *Humanisierung der Organisation: Wie man dem Menschen gerecht wird, indem man den Großteil seines Wesens ignoriert.* München: Vahlen.

McGivern, Gerry, and Ewan Ferlie. 2007. "Playing Tick-Box Games: Interrelating Defences in Professional Appraisal." *Human Relations* 60 (9): 1361–85. https://doi.org/10.1177/0018726707082851.

McGregor, Douglas. 1960. *The Human Side of Enterprise.* New York: McGraw-Hill.

McKenna, Steve, Lucia Garcia-Lorenzo, and Todd Bridgman. 2010. "Managing, Managerial Control and Managerial Identity in the Post-Bureaucratic World." *Journal of Management Development* 29 (2): 128–36. http://katalogplus.ub.uni-bielefeld.de/cgi-bin/new_titel.cgi?katkey=2010-01100-001~psyh&bestand=ext.

McSweeney, Brendan. 2006. "Are We Living in a Post-Bureaucratic Epoch?" *Journal of Organizational Change Management* 19 (1): 22–37. https://doi.org/10.1108/09534810610643668.

Merton, Robert K. 1936. "The Unanticipated Consequences of Purposive Social Action." *American Sociological Review* 1: 894–904.

Merton, Robert K. 1957. "Bureaucratic Structure and Personality." In *Social Theory and Social Structure*, edited by Robert K. Merton. 2nd ed., 195–206. Glencoe: Free Press.

Meyer, John W. 1992. "Institutionalization and the Rationality of Formal Organizational Structure." In *Organizational Environments: Ritual and Rationality*, edited by John W. Meyer and W. R. Scott, 261–83. Newbury/ London/ New Delhi: Sage.

Meyer, John W., and Brian Rowan. 1977. "Institutionalized Organizations. Formal Structure as Myth and Ceremony." *American Journal of Sociology* 83: 340–63.

Meyerhoff, Jeff. 2010. *Bald Ambition: A Critique of Ken Wilber's Theory of Everything:* Inside the Curtain Press.

Micklethwait, John, and Adrian Wooldridge. 1996. *The Witch Doctors: Making Sense of the Management Gurus.* London: William Heinemann.

Milgram, Stanley. 1974. *Obedience to Authority*. New York: Harper & Row.

Miller, Danny, and Joh Hartwick. 2002. "Spotting Management Fads." *Harvard Business Review* 80 (10): 26–27.

Miller, Danny, Jon Hartwick, and Isabelle Le Breton-Miller. 2004. "How to Detect a Management Fad—And Distinguish It from a Classic." *Business Horizons* 47 (4): 7–16. https://doi.org/10.1016/S0007-6813(04)00043-6.

Minnaar, Reinald, and Svenja van Vondelen. 2022. "Control in Holacratische Organisaties: Een Verkennend Onderzoek Naar De Controlmechanismen Achter Zelfsturing." *Maandblad voor Accountancy en Bedrijfseconomie* 96 (5/6): 133–43. https://doi.org/10.5117/mab.96.76851.

Mintzberg, Henry. 1980. "Structure in 5's: A Synthesis of the Research on Organization Design." *Management Science* 26 (3): 322–41. https://doi.org/10.1287/mnsc.26.3.322.

Mintzberg, Henry. 1983. *Structures in Fives: Designing Effective Organizations*.

Mintzberg, Henry. 1988. "The Adhocracy." In *The Strategy Process: Concepts, Contexts, and Cases*, edited by James B. Quinn, Henry Mintzberg, and Robert M. James, 607–27. Englewood Cliffs: Prentice-Hall.

Mintzberg, Henry, and Alexandra McHugh. 1985. "Strategy Formation in an Adhocracy." *Administrative Science Quarterly* 30: 180–97.

Mitterer, Gerald. 2015. "Holacracy - Ein Fleischwolf für rganisationale Entscheidungsprozesse." In *Management der Nonprofit-Organisation – Bewährte Instrumente im praktischen Einsatz.*, edited by Eschenbach, Meyer, Herbert Schober, and Horak, 426–32. Stuttgart: Schäffer-Poeschel.

Moe, Terry M. 1984. "The New Economics of Organizations." *American Journal of Political Science* 28: 739–77.

Mont, Simon. 2017. "Autopsy of a Failed Holacracy: Lessons in Justice, Equity, and Self-Management." https://nonprofitquarterly.org/2018/01/09/autopsy-failed-holacracy-lessons-justice-equity-self-management/.

Morgan, Gareth. 1986. *Images of Organization*. Beverly Hills: Sage.
Müller, Alexander O. 2019. *Reinhard Höhn: Ein Leben Zwischen Kontinuität und Neubeginn*. Berlin: be.bra.
Neal, Judi. 2013. *Creating Enlightened Organizations: Four Gateways to Spirit at Work*. New York: Palgrave Macmillan. https://ebookcentral.proquest.com/lib/kxp/detail.action?docID=5996275.
Nonaka, Ikujiro, and Hirotaka Takeuci. 1995. *The Knowledge Creating Company: How Japanese Companies Create the Dynamics of Innovation*. New York/ Oxford: Oxford University Press.
Noon, Mike, Geraldine Healy, Cynthia Forson, and Franklin Oikelome. 2013. "The Equality Effects of the 'Hyper-Formalization' of Selection." *Brit J Manage* 24 (3): 333–46. https://doi.org/10.1111/j.1467-8551.2011.00807.x.
Oane, Vlademir. 2016. "Holacracy and the Mirage of the Boss-Less Workplace: Lessons from the Failures at Github, Medium & Buffer." Medium. Link: https://medium.com/battle-room/holacracy-and-the-mirage-of-the-boss-less-workplace-lessons-from-the-failures-at-github-medium-4355993926d4#.sam1yaruk.
Oestereich, Bernd, and Claudia Schröder. 2017. *Das Kollegial geführte Unternehmen: Ideen und Praktiken für die agile Organisation von Morgen*. München: Vahlen.
O'Neill, Onora. 2010. *A Question of Trust*. 5th ed. Cambridge: Cambridge University Press.
Osrecki, Fran. 2015. "Fighting Corruption with Transparent Organizations: Anti-Corruption and Functional Deviance in Organizational Behavior." *Ephemera* 15: 337–64.
Ostroff, Frank. 1999. *The Horizontal Organization: What the Organization of the Future Looks Like and Now It Delivers Value to Customers*. New York: Oxford University Press. http://lib.myilibrary.com/detail.asp?id=52995.
Ouchi, William G. 1981. *Theory Z: How American Business Can Meet the Japanese Challenge*. New York: Addison-Wesley.
Paranque, Bernard, and Hugh Willmott. 2014. "Cooperatives—Saviours or Gravediggers of Capitalism? Critical Performativity and the John Lewis Partnership." *Organization* 21: 604–25.

Pasternack, Bruce A., and Albert J. Viscio. 1998. *The Centerless Corporation: Transforming Your Organization for Growth and Prosperity in the New Millennium.* New York: Simon & Schuster.

Peters, Thomas J. 1992. *Liberation Management: Necessary Disorganization for the Nanosecond Nineties.* New York: Knopf.

Peters, Thomas J., and Robert H. Waterman. 1982. *In Search of Excellence.* New York: Harper & Row.

Peters, Thomas J., and Robert H. Waterman. 1983. *Auf der Suche nach Spitzenleistungen.* Landsberg: Moderne Industrie.

Peters, Tom. 1988. *Thriving on Chaos: Handbook for a Management Revolution.* New York: Harper & Row.

Peters, Tom. 1993. *Jenseits der Hierarchien: Liberation Management.* Düsseldorf: Econ.

Peters, Vic. 2018. "The Relationship Between Roles and Authority." https://medium.com/@sandro997/the-relationship-between-roles-and-authority-9716e9a6d18c.

Pinchot, Gifford. 1988. *Intrapreneuring: Mitarbeiter als Unternehmer.* Wiesbaden: Gabler.

Prat, Andrea. 2005. "The Wrong Kind of Transparency." *American Economic Review* 95 (3): 862–77. https://doi.org/10.1257/0002828054201297.

Presthus, Robert V. 1961. "Weberian v. Welfare Bureaucracy in Traditional Society." *Administrative Science Quarterly* 6: 1–24.

Purser, Ronald E., and Steven Cabana. 1998. *The Self Managing Organization: How Leading Companies Are Transforming the Work of Teams for Real Impact.* New York: Free Press.

Rąb-Kettler, Karolina. 2018. "New Management Models as Reflection and Anticipation of Socio-Economic Changes." *SPSUTOM*, no. 122: 167–74. https://doi.org/10.29119/1641-3466.2018.122.18.

Ravarini, Aurelio, and Marcello Martinez. 2019. "Lost in Holacracy? The Possible Role of E-HRM in Dealing with the Deconstruction of Hierarchy." In *HRM 4.0 for Human-Centered Organizations*, edited by Rita Bissola and Barbara Imperatori, 63–79. Advanced series in management. Bingley: Emerald Publishing.

Reingold, Jennifer. 2016. "How a Radical Shift Left Zappos Reeling." http://fortune.com/zappos-tony-hsieh-holacracy/.

Reitzig, Markus. 2022. *Get Better at Flatter: A Guide to Shaping and Leading Organizations with Less Hierarchy*. Cham: Palgrave Macmillan.

Rhodes, Carl, and O. Milani Price. 2011. "The Post-Bureaucratic Parasite: Contrasting Narratives of Organizational Change in Local Government." *Management Learning* 42 (3): 241–60. https://doi.org/10.1177/1350507610385765.

Ringel, Leopold. 2018. "Unpacking the Transparency-Secrecy Nexus: Frontstage and Backstage Behaviour in a Political Party." *Organization Studies* 91:705-723. https://doi.org/10.1177/0170840618759817.

Roberts, Alasdair. 2006. "Dashed Expectations: Governmental Adaption to Transparency Rules." In *Transparency: The Key to Better Governance?* edited by Christoph Hood and David Heald, 107–25. Oxford: Oxford University Press.

Robertson, Brian J. 2006. "An Interview with Brian Robertson on Holacracy." http://library.uniteddiversity.coop.

Robertson, Brian J. 2012. "It's Just Good Business: Interview with Jeff Klein." www.entheos.com/radio/shows/Its-Just-Good-Business jetzt heoric.us.

Robertson, Brian J. 2014. "History of Holacracy." https://blog.holacracy.org/history-of-holacracy-c7a8489f8eca.

Robertson, Brian J. 2015a. *Holacracy: The New Management System for a Rapidly Changing World*. New York: Henry Holt.

Robertson, Brian J. 2015b. *Holacracy: The Revolutionary Management System That Abolishes Hierarchy*. London: Portfolio Penguin.

Robertson, Brian J. 2017. "The Humanity of Holacracy: 4 Ways Holacracy Brings Out the Best in People." https://blog.holacracy.org/holacracys-human-side-36d601882d21.

Robertson, Brian J. 2021. "Holacracy Mastermind Brian Robertson as Our Guest." https://www.linkedin.com/pulse/holacracy-mastermind-brian-robertson-our-guest-way-new-trautmann/.

Robertson, Brian J., Anthony Moquin, and Gareth Powell. 2009. "United States Patent Application Pubication. Method for Structuring and Controlling an Organization." https://patents.google.com/patent/US20090006113.

Rojot, Jacques. 2005. *Théorie Des Organisations*. 2e éd. Paris: Ed. Eska.

Rosenzweig, Phil. 2014. *The Halo Effect: ... And the Eight Other Business Delusions That Deceive Managers*. Riverside: Free Press.

Salaman, Graeme. 2005. "Bureaucracy and Beyond: Managers and Leaders in the "Post-Bureaucratic" Organization." In *The Values of Bureaucracy*, edited by Paul Du Gay, 141–63. Oxford/ New York: Oxford University Press.

Schell, Sabrina, and Nicole Bischof. 2022. "Change the Way of Working. Ways into Self-organization with the Use of Holacracy: An Empirical Investigation." *European Management Review* 19:123–37. https://doi.org/10.1111/emre.12457.

Schluchter, Wolfgang. 1985. *Aspekte bürokratischer Herrschaft: Studien zur Interpretation der fortschreitenden Industriegesellschaft*. Frankfurt a.M. Suhrkamp.

Seabright, Mark A., and Jacques Delacroix. 1996. "The Minimalist Organization as a Postbureaucratic Form." *Journal of Management Inquiry* 5:140–54. https://doi.org/10.1177/105649269652007.

Selznick, Philip. 1943. "An Approach to a Theory of Bureaucracy." *American Sociological Review* 8: 47–54.

Selznick, Philip. 1949. *TVA and the Grass Roots*. Berkeley: University of California Press.

Semler, Ricardo. 1995. *Das Semco System*. München: Heyne.

Senge, Peter M. 1990. *The Fifth Discipline: The Art and Practice of the Learning Organization*. New York: Doubleday.

Sherif, Muzafer, O. J. Harvey, B. Jack White, William R. Hood, and Carolyn W. Sherif. 1988. *The Robbers Cave Experiment: Intergroup Conflict and Cooperation*. Middletown: Wesleyan University Press. http://search.ebscohost.com/login.aspx?direct=true&scope=site&db=nlebk&db=nlabk&AN=370634.

Simon, Herbert A. 1965. "The Architecture of Complexity." *General Systems* 10: 63–76.

Sisodia, Rajendra S., David B. Wolfe, and Jagdish N. Sheth. 2010. *Firms of Endearment: How World-Class Companies Profit from Passion and Purpose*. Upper Saddle River: Wharton School Publisher.

Smiles, Tom, and Gareth A. S. Edwards. 2021. "How Does Extinction Rebellion Engage with Climate Justice? A Case Study of XR Norwich." *Local Environment* 26:1445–60. https://doi.org/10.1080/1 3549839.2021.1974367.

Smith, Chris. 2015. "Rediscovery of the Labour Process." In *The SAGE Handbook of the Sociology of Work and Employment*, edited by Stephen Edgell, Heidi Gottfried, and Edward Granter, 205–24. London: Sage.

Spencer, David A. 2000. "Braverman and the Contribution of Labour Process Analysis to the Critique of Capitalist Production - Twenty-Five Years on." *Work, Employment & Society* 14 (2): 223–43.

Starbuck, William H. 1988. "Surmounting Our Human Limitations." In *Paradox and Transformation: Toward a Theory of Change in Organization and Management*, edited by Robert E. Quinn and Kim S. Cameron, 65–80. Cambridge: Ballinger.

Stinchcombe, Arthur L. 1959. "Bureaucratic and Craft Administration of Production: A Comparative Study." *Administrative Science Quarterly* 4: 168–87.

Stone, Christopher D. 1975. *Where the Law Ends: The Social Control of Corporate Behaviour*. New York: Harper & Row.

Strothotte, Adrian. 2023. "Purpose und Selbstorganisation: Über Funktionen und Folgen von Zwecken in holakratischen Organisationen." In *Holacracy: Funktionen und Folgen eines Managementmodells*, edited by Stefan Kühl und Sua-Ngam-Iam. Wiesbaden: Springer Gabler.

Sua-Ngam-Iam, Phanmika. 2023a. "Anhang - Zur Methodischen Vorgehensweise." In *Holacracy: Funktionen und Folgen eines Managementmodells*, edited by Stefan Kühl und Sua-Ngam-Iam. Wiesbaden: Springer Gabler.

Sua-Ngam-Iam, Phanmika. 2023b. "Tauschgeschäfte: Das Verhältnis von Formalität und Informalität in der holakratischen Organisation." In *Holacracy: Funktionen und Folgen eines Managementmodells*, edited by Stefan Kühl und Sua-Ngam-Iam. Wiesbaden: Springer Gabler.

Sua-Ngam-Iam, Phanmika, and Stefan Kühl. 2021. "Das Wuchern Der Formalstruktur." *Journal für Psychologie* 29: 39–71.

Taylor, Frederick W. 1967. *The Principles of Scientific Management*. London: Norton.
Taylor, William C., and Polly G. LaBarre. 2006. *Mavericks at Work: Why the Most Original Minds in Business Win*. New York: William Morrow.
Thompson, James D. 1967. *Organizations in Action*. New York: McGraw-Hill.
Thompson, Victor A. 1961. "Hierarchy, Specialization, and Organizational Conflict." *Administrative Science Quarterly* 5: 485–521.
Tichy, Noel M. 1995. *Regieanweisung für Revolutionäre: Unternehmenswandel in drei Akten*. Frankfurt a.M./ New York: Campus.
Tincup, William. 2014. "The Six Problems with Holacracy." http://fistfuloftalent.com/2014/01/six-problems-holacracy.html.
Toffler, Alvin. 1971. *Future Shock*. New York: Bantam Book.
Torbert, William R. 2004. *Action Inquiry: The Secret of Timely and Transforming Leadership*. San Francisco: Berrett-Koehler Publishers. https://learning.oreilly.com/library/view/-/9781605096339/?ar.
Turco, Catherine. 2016. *The Conversational Firm: Rethinking Bureaucracy in the Age of Social Media*. The middle range. New York: Columbia University Press. https://search.ebscohost.com/login.aspx?direct=true&scope=site&db=nlebk&db=nlabk&AN=1341921.
Udy, Stanley H. 1959. ""Bureaucracy" and "Rationality" in Weber's Organization Theory." *American Sociological Review* 24: 591–95.
Urwick, Lyndall F. 1943. *The Elements of Administration*. New York: Harper & Brothers.
Välikangas, Lisa. 2010. *The Resilient Organization: How Adaptive Cultures Thrive Even When Strategy Fails*. New York: McGraw-Hill.
Veuve, Alain. 2017. "Holacracy - Aber …". https://www.aoe.com/de/blog/holacracy-aber-000586.html.
Warnecke, Hans-Jürgen. 1992. *Die fraktale Fabrik: Revolution der Unternehmenskultur*. Berlin: Springer.
Weber, Max. 1976. *Wirtschaft und Gesellschaft*. Tübingen: J.C.B. Mohr.
Wenger, Etienne C. 1999. *Communities of Practice: Learning, Meaning, and Identity*. Zur Einführung. Cambridge/ New York: Cambridge University Press.

Wenger, Etienne C., and William M. Snyder. 2000. "Communities of Practice. The Organizational Frontier." *Harvard Business Review* 1 (2): 139–45.
Wilber, Ken. 1995. *Sex, Ecology, Spirituality: The Spirit of Evolution.* Boston: Shambhala.
Wilber, Ken. 2000. *A Theory of Everything: An Integral Vision of Politics, Science and Spiruality.* Boston: Shambhala.
Wilber, Ken. 2006. "What We Are, That We See." http://www.kenwilber.com/blog/show/46.
Wildemann, Horst. 1988. *Die modulare Fabrik: Kundennahe Produktion durch Fertigungssegmentierung.* München: TCW.
Willke, Helmut. 1989. *Systemtheorie entwickelter Gesellschaften: Dynamik und Riskanz moderner Gesellschaftlicher Selbstorganisation.* Weinheim: Juventa.
Wittrock, Dennis. 2007. "Was heißt "Integrale Organisation"? Soziokratie, Holakratie und die Evolution menschlicher Organisationsformen." *integrale perspektiven* (5): 4–11.
Wittrock, Dennis. 2020. "Geleitwort." In *Integrale Führung: Wie Sie mit neuen Ansätzen sich Selbst, Teams und Unternehmen entwickeln*, edited by Heike Kuhlmann and Sandra Horn, v–vii. Wiesbaden: SpringerGabler.
Wittrock, Dennis. 2021. "Kommentar zu Adrian Strothottes Artikel "Mit Holacracy zur Purpose Driven Organization? Über die Grenzen eines Organisationsmodells"." https://denniswittrock.com/2021/02/23/kommentar-zu-adrian-strothottes-artikel-mit-holacracy-zur-purpose-driven-organization-ueber-die-grenzen-eines-organisationsmodells/.
Witzel, Morgen. 2012. *A History of Management Thought.* Business and management. London: Routledge.
Wolfe, Norman. 2011. *The Living Organization: Transforming Business to Create Extraordinary:* Quantum Leaders Publishing.
Womack, James P., Daniel T. Jones, and Daniel Ross. 1990. *The Machine That Changed the World.* New York: Maxwell Macmillan International.
Wood, Stephen, and John Kelly. 1982. "Taylorism, Responsible Autonomy and Management Strategy." In *The Degradation of Work? Skill,*

Deskilling and the Labour Process: Skill, Deskilling and the Labour Process, edited by Stephen Wood, 74–89. London: Hutchinson.

Xpreneurs. 2021. *Holacracy® Verfassung: Version 5.0 - DE:* xpreneurs.

Yugendhar, Akkinapally, and Syed Mahamood Ali. 2017. "Evaluation of Implementing Holacracy: A Comprehensive Study on Zappos." *International Journal of Engineering and Management Research* 7: 163–71. https://www.indianjournals.com/ijor.aspx?target=ijor:ijemr&volume=7&issue=5&article=027.

Zeleny, Milan. 1989. "Sociocracy." *Human System Management* 8: 245–48.

Zeuch, Andreas. 2016a. "Holacracy: Eine kurze Analyse der Fallbeispiele." https://unternehmensdemokraten.de/2016/12/19/holacracy-eine-kurze-analyse-der-fallbeispiele/.

Zeuch, Andreas. 2016b. "Holacracy: Vom Scheitern eines Betriebssystems." https://www.unternehmensdemokraten.de/holacracy-vom-scheitern-eines-betriebssystems/.

Zimbardo, Philip G. *The Lucifer Effect: Understanding How Good People Turn Evil.* London: Rider, 2007. http://www.youtube.com/watch?v=9xpsVlY3QQc.

www.ingramcontent.com/pod-product-compliance
Lightning Source LLC
Chambersburg PA
CBHW031156020426
42333CB00013B/691